C000005059

THE AMERICAN LUTHERAN THEOLOGICAL JOURNAL
Summer 2015
Volume 2 Number 1

CONTENTS

Articles

Book Reviews....67

Sermon

An Exegetical and Theological Exploration of Ephesians 2:1-10
By Chris Rosebrough

Introduction
Ephesians 2:1-10 is arguably one of the most important passages in all of scripture that pertains to the doctrines of Original Sin and Justification. This passage of scripture explicitly describes mankind's state prior to God's saving acts as "dead in trespasses and sins" and clearly and unequivocally declares that salvation is God's work, not ours, and it is by God's grace through faith and not as a result of our works. This portion of scripture also provides a succinct yet profound way of understanding the role of good works in the Christian life. Paul's argument in this passage is compact, yet has a surprising depth to it.

Translation
1 Καὶ ὑμᾶς ὄντας νεκροὺς τοῖς παραπτώμασιν καὶ ταῖς ἁμαρτίαις ὑμῶν

> You also (were raised to life) when you were dead in your trespasses and sins

2 ἐν αἷς ποτε περιεπατήσατε κατὰ τὸν αἰῶνα τοῦ κόσμου τούτου, κατὰ τὸν ἄρχοντα τῆς ἐξουσίας τοῦ ἀέρος, τοῦ πνεύματος τοῦ νῦν ἐνεργοῦντος ἐν τοῖς υἱοῖς τῆς ἀπειθείας·

> in which you conducted your life according to this age of the world, according to the ruler of the power of the air, the spirit now working in the sons of disobedience.

3 ἐν οἷς καὶ ἡμεῖς πάντες ἀνεστράφημέν ποτε ἐν ταῖς ἐπιθυμίαις τῆς σαρκὸς ἡμῶν ποιοῦντες τὰ θελήματα τῆς σαρκὸς καὶ τῶν διανοιῶν, καὶ ἤμεθα τέκνα φύσει ὀργῆς ὡς καὶ οἱ λοιποί·

> among them we also all formerly conducted ourselves in the desires of our flesh, doing the will of the flesh and the mind, and we were by nature children of wrath as also the rest.

4 ὁ δὲ θεὸς πλούσιος ὢν ἐν ἐλέει, διὰ τὴν πολλὴν ἀγάπην αὐτοῦ ἣν ἠγάπησεν ἡμᾶς,

> but God who is rich in mercy, through his great love which he loved us

5 καὶ ὄντας ἡμᾶς νεκροὺς τοῖς παραπτώμασιν συνεζωοποίησεν τῷ Χριστῷ, - χάριτί ἐστε σεσῳσμένοι –

> and we being dead in trespasses he (God) made us alive together with Christ – by grace you have been saved

6 καὶ συνήγειρεν καὶ συνεκάθισεν ἐν τοῖς ἐπουρανίοις ἐν Χριστῷ Ἰησοῦ,

> and he (God) raised us up together with (him) and seated us with (him) in the heavenlies, in Christ Jesus.

7 ἵνα ἐνδείξηται ἐν τοῖς αἰῶσιν τοῖς ἐπερχομένοις τὸ ὑπερβάλλον πλοῦτος τῆς χάριτος αὐτοῦ ἐν χρηστότητι ἐφ᾽ ἡμᾶς ἐν Χριστῷ Ἰησοῦ.

> In order that he might demonstrate in the coming ages the surpassing riches of his grace in kindness toward us in Christ Jesus

8 Τῇ γὰρ χάριτί ἐστε σεσῳσμένοι διὰ πίστεως· καὶ τοῦτο οὐκ ἐξ ὑμῶν, θεοῦ τὸ δῶρον·

> For by grace you have been saved through faith, and this not from yourselves, (it is) the gift of God,

9 οὐκ ἐξ ἔργων, ἵνα μή τις καυχήσηται.

> Not from works, in order that no one might boast

10 αὐτοῦ γάρ ἐσμεν ποίημα, κτισθέντες ἐν Χριστῷ Ἰησοῦ ἐπὶ ἔργοις ἀγαθοῖς οἷς προητοίμασεν ὁ θεός, ἵνα ἐν αὐτοῖς περιπατήσωμεν.

> For we are his creation, created in Christ Jesus for good works which God prepared beforehand that we might conduct our lives in them.

Textual and Grammatical Notes

2:1   ὑμᾶς is in the accusative, not the nominitive. Find its verb is critical to a correct translation.

2:3   ἀναστρέφω appears as an aorist passive participle. BDAG provides two possible definitions when ἀναστρέφω is a passive. The first is to "spend time in a locality, *stay, live*". The second is to "to conduct oneself in terms of certain principles, *act, behave, conduct oneself, live.*[1] Given the context, Paul is not referring to living in a geographic location, nor does he seem to be describing living in general. Instead, he is describing the type of living that pertains to how one conducts himself. Therefore, translating ἀνεστράφημέν as "lived" is too weak of a translation and doesn't sufficiently capture what Paul saying.

2:5   συζωοποιέω appears only twice in the New Testament. The other occurrence in Colossians 2:13 clearly references baptism. There are two notable textual variants in this verse. First, the reading from 𝔓[46], B, 33, is συνεζωοποίησεν ἐν τῷ Χριστῷ.[2]
Second, "the reading χάριτι immediately after τῷ Χριστῷ appears in the Alexandrian manuscripts, ℵ, B, and in many Byzantine manuscripts. It therefore has early and wide attestation and is, with the highest probability and with virtually no controversy, the correct reading. The two variations from this reading come from late manuscripts, and each is limited to a single text type."[3]

Analysis

Although Paul's argument in this passage does not appear to be formally chiastic, the opening portion of this passage and the

---

[1] Walter Bauer, Frederick W. Danker, William Arndt, and F.W. Gingrich. *A Greek-English Lexicon of the New Testament and Other Early Christian Literature* (Chicago: University of Chicago Press, 2000), 72.

[2] Frank Thielman, *Ephesians*, Baker Exegetical Commentary on the New Testament (Grand Rapids, MI: Baker Academic, 2010), 140. "If this were correct, it would be exegetically significant since συνεζωοποίησεν would then refer not to the union of Christians with Christ's new life but to the union of Christians whom, together, God had made alive "in Christ." It might then anticipate the theme of the unity of Gentile and Jewish Christians in 2:11–22. "The concentration of the manuscripts with this reading in the Alexandrian text type and the lateness of the Western witnesses, however, make this reading a poor choice in comparison to the simple τῷ Χριστῷ, which appears in early Alexandrian (ℵ, A) as well as Western (D, F, G) and Byzantine witnesses (L, and a range of minuscules).[24] The additional ἐν arose either as an echo of ἐν Χριστῷ Ἰησοῦ at the end of 2:6, or (more probably, since the phrase in 2:6 comes later) from a mistaken repetition of the final syllable of the preceding συνεζωοποίησεν."
[3] Ibid.

description of mankind prior to salvation has a mirror opposite description described for Christians in the second half of this text.

Part one of Paul's contrasting descriptions begins with a description of man's state as a result of the fall and the condition in which every human finds himself prior to God's regenerative work through the word and sacraments. Said Paul, "You also (were raised to life) when you were dead in your trespasses and sins in which you conducted your life according to this age of the world, according to the ruler of the power of the air, the spirit now working in the sons of disobedience." Verse one opens with Καὶ ὑμᾶς and "you" is not in the nominative case but is instead, in the accusative. Therefore, it is not functioning as the subject of Paul's thought. F.F. Bruce, commenting on this verse wrote:

> "You" at the beginning of v. 1 probably means "you Gentiles," over against "we also"—that is to say, we Jews—in v. 3. "You" stands in the accusative case, but there is no expressed verb to which it forms the object. The verb implied is either "raised" as in Eph. 1:20 (God not only raised Christ from the dead; he raised "you also") or (more probably) "brought to life" in v. 5 below. In the latter case the construction begun in v. 1 is broken off after the succession of adjective clauses, and the sense is resumed with the new sentence "But God ..." in vv. 4 and 5.[4]

Translating verse one as "you also (were raised to life) when you were dead in your trespasses" not only more accurately conveys the grammar of verse 1, it more accurately captures the thrust of the distinction that Paul is making in this passage. It is the distinction between being dead in trespasses and sins and what it means to conduct your life (περιεπατήσατε[5] in verse 2) as a dead person in contrast to being alive in Christ and what it means to conduct your life (περιπατήσωμεν in verse 10) as a one who has been made alive by God.

Paul's use of περιπατέω in both verse 2 and verse 10 is describing how a person holistically lives his life[6]. Andrew Lincoln, in

---

[4] F. F. Bruce, *The Epistles to the Colossians, to Philemon, and to the Ephesians*, The New International Commentary on the New Testament (Grand Rapids, MI: Wm. B. Eerdmans Publishing Co., 1984), 280.

[5] περιπατέω means to conduct one's life, *comport oneself, behave, live* as habit of conduct. Translating περιπατέω as 'walk' does not sufficiently capture what Paul is describing in this passage. See BDAG, 803.

[6] Thielman, "In the Pauline corpus, the term is nearly always followed by a prepositional phrase, an adverbial phrase, or a word in the dative case that

his commentary on Ephesians argues that Paul's use of the word περιπατέω is a Hebraism. Lincoln said:

> περιπατεῖν, literally, "to walk" (cf. also v 10), is a Hebraism common in the LXX in translating הלך, *hālak*, in its use for ethical conduct or a way of living. The rabbis, of course, used this terminology in speaking of teaching about ethical conduct—*hălākâ*. The use of περιπατεῖν in this sense in the NT is most characteristic of Paul's writings but also occurs in the Johannine literature.[7]

With this understanding of περιπατέω, it is clear that Paul is saying that how a person conducts his life is determined by whether or not he is dead or alive. If he is dead in trespasses and sins then his conduct, his way of life is "according to this age of the world, according to the ruler of the power of the air, the spirit now working in the sons of disobedience." In other words, one who is dead in trespasses and sins is completely under the control, dominion, influence and power of the devil.

Describing unbelievers as dead does not originate with Paul. Jesus spoke this way as well. Matthew 8:22 says, "And Jesus said to him, "Follow me, and leave the dead to bury their own dead." In John 5:24 Jesus states, "Truly, truly, I say to you, whoever hears my word and believes him who sent me has eternal life. He does not come into judgment, but has passed from death to life."

Paul then continues to describe what it means to conduct one's life as one who is dead in trespasses and sins. Paul says, "[A]mong them we also all formerly conducted ourselves in the desires of our flesh, doing the will of the flesh and the mind, and we were by nature children of wrath as also the rest." It is significant that Paul switches from the personal pronouns ὑμᾶς and ὑμῶν (you) in verse 1 to ἡμεῖς (we) in verse 3. This signifies that both Jews, with whom Paul was numbered, and gentiles, with whom the Ephesian Christians were numbered, were born under the dominion of the devil and like the rest of mankind were by nature children of wrath. Paul's words from Romans 3:9–18 dovetail perfectly with his thought in this verse.

---

more closely identifies the mode of living to which the word refers (Seesemann, *TDNT* 5:944; BDAG 803). Here Paul uses three such phrases." (123)

[7] Andrew T. Lincoln, *Ephesians*, vol. 42, Word Biblical Commentary (Dallas: Word, Incorporated, 1990), 94.

What then? Are we Jews any better off? No, not at all. For we have already charged that all, both Jews and Greeks, are under sin, as it is written: "None is righteous, no, not one; no one understands; no one seeks for God. All have turned aside; together they have become worthless; no one does good, not even one." "Their throat is an open grave; they use their tongues to deceive." "The venom of asps is under their lips." "Their mouth is full of curses and bitterness." "Their feet are swift to shed blood; in their paths are ruin and misery, and the way of peace they have not known." "There is no fear of God before their eyes."

Paul's point is that all of humanity is dead in trespasses and sins *by nature.* This is the result of Adam and Eve's rebellion and fall into sin and the consequences of their sin are cataclysmic. No human is exempt and no human is free. All of humanity is born under the rule of the devil, dead in trespasses and sins with the result that we all naturally "conducted ourselves in the desires of our flesh, doing the will of the flesh (ἐπιθυμίαις τῆς σαρκὸς) and the mind."

Paul does not unpack what the will of the flesh (ἐπιθυμίαις τῆς σαρκὸς) is in this passage. But, he does begin to unpack this idea latter in this epistle. In Ephesians 4:17–19 he writes,

Now this I say and testify in the Lord, that you must no longer walk (περιπατεῖν) as the Gentiles do, in the futility of their minds. They are darkened in their understanding, alienated from the life of God because of the ignorance that is in them, due to their hardness of heart. They have become callous and have given themselves up to sensuality, greedy to practice every kind of impurity." Then in Ephesians 5:3–10 Paul says, "But sexual immorality and all impurity or covetousness must not even be named among you, as is proper among saints. Let there be no filthiness nor foolish talk nor crude joking, which are out of place, but instead let there be thanksgiving. For you may be sure of this, that everyone who is sexually immoral or impure, or who is covetous (that is, an idolater), has no inheritance in the kingdom of Christ and God. Let no one deceive you with empty words, for because of these things the wrath of God comes upon the sons of disobedience. Therefore do not become partners with them; for at one time you were darkness, but now you are light in the Lord. Walk as children of light (for the fruit of light is found in all that is good and right and true), and try to discern what is pleasing to the Lord.

When we compare Ephesians 5:3–10 and Ephesians 4:17–19 with Galatians 5:16–21 we see an almost perfect consistency in Paul's theology.[8] When he writes about what it means to conduct your life according to the desires of the flesh. Paul says,

> But I say, walk (περιπατεῖτε) by the Spirit, and you will not gratify the desires of the flesh (ἐπιθυμίαν σαρκὸς). For the desires of the flesh (σὰρξ ἐπιθυμεῖ) are against the Spirit, and the desires of the Spirit are against the flesh, for these are opposed to each other, to keep you from doing the things you want to do. But if you are led by the Spirit, you are not under the law. Now the works of the flesh are evident: sexual immorality, impurity, sensuality, idolatry, sorcery, enmity, strife, jealousy, fits of anger, rivalries, dissensions, divisions, envy, drunkenness, orgies, and things like these.

By unpacking what Paul is speaking about when he describes those who conduct their lives "according to this age of the world, according to the ruler of the power of the air... in the desires of our flesh, doing the will of the flesh," we are able to understand just how desperate our situation is as those who are born dead in trespasses and sins. To be a child of wrath by nature, under the dominion of the devil results in a conduct of life where we are utterly sold out to fulfilling the desires of the flesh. This means that our default way of living, under the devil's power, is marked by "sexual immorality, impurity, sensuality, idolatry, sorcery, enmity, strife, jealousy, fits of anger, rivalries, dissensions, divisions, envy, drunkenness, orgies, and things like these." This is a bleak description of all of humanity. But, as painful as this description is, Paul tells us the truth about our condition.

It is also significant that Paul, in describing our conduct, not only describes it as following the desires of the flesh but also the desires of the mind. This makes it clear that our corruption is total and does not merely impact a portion of our being, it also makes it clear from Paul's other works where he discusses our mind and flesh that we cannot work our way out of this condition by choosing to submit to

---

[8] This is strong evidence for Pauline authorship of Ephesians. Consistency of thought and theology across multiple letters is practically impossible for a forger to pull off.

God's law rather than the devil. Paul says in Romans 8:7–8, "For the mind that is set on the flesh is hostile to God, for it does not submit to God's law; *indeed, it cannot.* Those who are in the flesh cannot please God."

Considering the depth and the magnitude of our problem as a race, revealed in this passage of scripture, it is clear that the Lutheran Reformers rightly understood this text when they formulated the Doctrine of Original as found in Article II of the Augsburg Confession:

> ### II. [Original Sin]
> [1] It is also taught among us that since the fall of Adam all men who are born according to the course of nature are conceived and born in sin. That is, all men are full of evil lust and inclinations from their mothers' wombs and are unable by nature to have true fear of God and true faith in God.
>
> [2] Moreover, this inborn sickness and hereditary sin is truly sin and condemns to the eternal wrath of God all those who are not born again through Baptism and the Holy Spirit.
>
> [3] Rejected in this connection are the Pelagians and others who deny that original sin is sin, for they hold that natural man is made righteous by his own powers, thus disparaging the sufferings and merit of Christ[9]

Not only does this article rightly explain, "all men who are born according to the course of nature are conceived and born in sin" it also explains that "all men are full of evil lust and inclinations from their mothers' wombs." These words echo Paul's words from this passage when he describes the result of our condition as we "conducted ourselves in the desires of our flesh, doing the will of the flesh and the mind." The term used by the Lutheran Reformers for this continual inclination and pursuing of sinful and sensual desires is *concupiscence* and it played a crucial role in the controversy with the Roman Catholic Church over the Lutheran contention that justification is by grace through faith alone. The reason why this is so critical to get right is that if one misdiagnoses mankind's problem as it pertains to his fallen state then one will necessarily prescribe the wrong solution. Melanchthon, in the Apology of the Augsburg Confession argues that the Roman Catholics in their Confutation, by not properly understanding

---

[9] Theodore G. Tappert, ed., *The Book of Concord the Confessions of the Evangelical Lutheran Church.* (Philadelphia: Mühlenberg Press, 1959), 29.

concupiscence and its theological implications, were, in a very real sense, denying what scripture, and more specifically what Paul reveals in Ephesians 2:1-10 regarding Original Sin. Melanchthon says:

> [6] To show our disagreement with this evil doctrine, we made mention of concupiscence; with the best of intentions we named it and explained it as a disease since human nature is born full of corruption and faults.
>
> [7] We have mentioned not only concupiscence but also the absence of the fear of God and of faith. We have done this because the scholastics misunderstand the patristic definition of original sin and therefore minimize original sin. They argue that the inclination to evil is a quality of the body; in their awkward way they ask whether it came through contact with the apple or through the serpent's breath, and whether medicine can cure it. By such questions they miss the main issue.
>
> [8] Thus when they talk about original sin, they do not mention the more serious faults of human nature, namely, ignoring God, despising him, lacking fear and trust in him, hating his judgment and fleeing it, being angry at him, despairing of his grace, trusting in temporal things, etc. These evils, which are most contrary to the law of God, the scholastics do not even mention. They even attribute to human nature unimpaired power to love God above all things and to obey his commandments "according to the substance of the act." And they do not see the contradiction.
>
> [9] To be able to love God above all things by one's own power and to obey his commandments, what else is this but to have original righteousness?[10]

Melanchthon's argument is thoroughly Pauline and accurately reflects Paul's thoughts in Ephesians 2 as well as Romans 3, 5 and 8. If humans have the power within themselves to love God above all things, then they are not truly under the power of the devil and are not by nature objects of God's wrath. Instead, as Melanchthon rightly points out, rather than suffering from original sin, they instead have original righteousness.

It is vital to understand that rightly understanding Ephesians 2:1-10 and particularly verses 1-3 is not merely an academic exercise.

---

[10] 101–102.

From a pastoral point of view, rightly teaching and preaching this passages and others as it pertains to the doctrine of Original Sin is ultimately not about making sure that your doctrinal i's are dotted and t's are crossed. Misunderstanding this passage and miscommunicating the depth of mankind's sinful condition opens the door for self-improvement theologies and self-justification schemes of every sort. The end result of every self-improvement theology, by necessity, is psychological despair and no ability to have an assurance of one's salvation. The tragic irony is that if one does not rightly understand the magnitude and depth of our sinful condition and they strike out to earn a right standing before God. Regardless of the rigor of the religious program they've enrolled in, they will not only have no assurance of salvation and no true sense of peace with God, but the will ultimately discover that the reason for that was because they were still children of wrath. As Paul states, "You are severed from Christ, you who would be justified by the law; you have fallen away from grace." (Galatians 5:4) In other words, a pastor as a servant of the word and a servant of those whom God has called him care for, is by necessity, not caring for the members of his congregation if he does not, through texts like this one, properly communicate the magnitude and hopeless reality of our sinful condition. If a pastor gets this wrong, and mistakenly preaches that humans are not utterly dead in their trespasses and sins and under the power of the devil, then he will, by necessity of human blindness and the law written on our hearts (*opinio legis*[11]) falsely teach that our right standing before God depends on our will, our efforts, and our works. In other words, Ephesians 2:1-10 is ground zero for the pastoral ministry. How a pastor understands this text will impact how he understands every other text of scripture and will either cause him to preach people to faith in Christ for eternal life or to strive for and earn their salvation and by doing so lead them to eternal damnation.

But God...

In Ephesians 2:4, Paul lets loose a Gospel thunderbolt when he writes "but God" (ὁ δὲ θεὸς). In this verse there is an abrupt change in the subject of the verbs. In verse one, Paul begins by talking about *you*

---

[11] Pieper, 13. "Because of the *opinio legis* inherent in man, the religion of all unbelievers is the religion of works. Moreover, there is in no man the "striving" after the way to life which the Christian religion offers, salvation through faith in Christ, crucified for the sins of the world. The way of grace is unknown to man."

gentiles (ὑμᾶς) and by verse three had expanded that to everyone, Jews and gentiles alike by using the word *we* (ἡμεῖς).

You were dead in your trespasses and sins.
You were dead in your trespasses and sins.
You conducted your life according to this age of the world.
We conducted ourselves in the desires of our flesh.
We did the will of the flesh and the mind.
We were by nature children of wrath.
But God...

Expecting, now to hear from God a verdict pronouncing us guilty before Him and our being sentenced to the fires of hell (which is exactly what we deserve), the words that follow are startling. Paul writes, "[B]ut God who is rich in mercy, through his great love with which he loved us and we being dead in trespasses He (God) made us alive together with Christ – by grace you have been saved —" There is no way of escaping it. The verb συνεζωοποίησεν can have only one subject and that subject is the nominative ὁ θεὸς. This God who is rich in mercy through the great love that he has for us, even when we were dead in our trespasses and sins, He has made us alive together with Christ! Thielman describes this unexpected turn this way:

> With the phrase ὁ δὲ θεός (*ho de theos*, but God), Paul now begins to describe God's response to the seemingly hopeless plight into which sin, the flesh, the mind, and the demonic world have plunged humanity (2:1–3). Although Paul and his readers deserve God's wrath (v. 3), God has made it possible for them to escape this otherwise inevitable destiny and to share Christ's victory over evil (vv. 5–6).[12]

Lenksi, in his commentary is compelled to worship God in light of this unexpected good news:

> "God, being rich in mercy," describes him according to his motive; the διά phrase modifies the three verbs and describes this motive still further as causing the threefold act. "Rich" in mercy brings out the sufficiency in God.

> Paul uses the three terms: ἔλεος—ἀγάπη—χάρις. While they are synonymous, each is distinctive, and the three are not to be

---

[12] Thielman, 132.

confused by ignoring this distinction. "Love" is the broadest: as in 1:4, it is the love of fullest comprehension and corresponding purpose. It sees our deadness and is moved to bring us to life. This divine, infinite love will ever remain the most wondrous and glorious mystery which is too deep for full penetration by our finite minds: "God is love," is so revealed to us in the gospel. *Let us fall down before him and adore the glory of his love.*

"Grace" is this love as it is extended to us sinners in our *guilt* and unworthiness and pardons the guilt for Christ's sake in spite of our unworthiness. "Mercy" goes out to the *wretched* and miserable. Grace deals with the cause, the guilt; mercy with the consequences, the wretched death in which we lie. All three are active in our restoration. Paul names them in the proper order. Having described us in our pitiful deadness, mercy is applied in order to remove this consequence of guilt; it is the mercy of love with its full knowledge and blessed purpose; and this love also in the form of grace as wiping out our guilt and its penalty of death. Here Paul again presents all the angles; his readers are to see them all.[13]

God did all of this to us and for us because of his great love, mercy, and grace. These two verses alone rule out any notion of merit or salvation via works either in whole or in part.

It is significant to note that F.F. Bruce's commentary opens up the question of when we were made alive together with Christ. Said F.F. Bruce:

> We were dead through our trespasses, says Paul (Jews and Gentiles alike), but from that state of death God brought us to life with Christ. Paul does teach elsewhere that believers in Christ "have been brought from death to life" with him (e.g., in Rom. 6:13), but there the death from which they have been brought to life is their death with Christ. Through faith-union with him they have died with him to their old existence and come alive with him to a new existence. "If we have died with Christ, we believe that we shall also live with him" (Rom. 6:8). Similarly in Colossians, "you were raised with Christ" (3:1) is the sequel to "you died with Christ" (2:20). But in Ephesians to

---

[13] R. C. H. Lenski, *The Interpretation of St. Paul's Epistles to the Galatians, to the Ephesians and to the Philippians* (Columbus, O.: Lutheran Book Concern, 1937), 414–415.

be raised with Christ is the sequel to being spiritually dead—to death through trespasses rather than to death with Christ.[14]

In his comment, Bruce, rightly, identifies a verbal connection with other portions of the Pauline corpus, namely: Romans 6:8 and Colossians 3:1. However, it is important to note that in both verses cited by Bruce as parallels to Ephesians 2:5 the referent to our union with Christ in His death and His resurrection is not faith. Instead, it is our baptism. Romans 6:8 reads, "Now if we have died with Christ, we believe that we will also live with him." But, the referent earlier in the same chapter reads, "Do you not know that all of us who have been baptized into Christ Jesus were baptized into his death? We were buried therefore with him by baptism into death, in order that, just as Christ was raised from the dead by the glory of the Father, we too might walk in newness of life." (Romans 6:3–4) It is the same with Colossians 3:1 which reads, "If then you have been raised with Christ, seek the things that are above, where Christ is, seated at the right hand of God." However, in Colossians 3:1 Paul is referencing what he has already made clear earlier in Colossians 2:11–13 which reads,

> In him also you were circumcised with a circumcision made without hands, by putting off the body of the flesh, by the circumcision of Christ, *having been buried with him in baptism,* in which you were also raised with him through faith in the powerful working of God, who raised him from the dead. And you, who were dead in your trespasses and the uncircumcision of your flesh, God made alive together with him (συζωοποιέω), having forgiven us all our trespasses...

In other words, Paul in Ephesians 2:5 does not explicitly mention baptism as the means by which we're made alive together with Christ. But, by using the verb συζωοποιέω he is, in a very real sense, pointing the Ephesian Christians back to their baptism. F.F. Bruce clearly sees the correlation to the right passages but doesn't rightly draw the full connection back to baptism. Even Thielman sees the connection between Ephesians 2:5 and Colosians 2:13 but is unable to make the connection to baptism despite the fact that Colossians 2:13 is clearly referring to baptism. Thielman writes:

> "The first verb, συζωοποιέω (*syzōopoieō,* make alive together with), appears only here and in the closely related Col. 2:13 in

---

[14] Bruce, 285–286.

all known Greek literature prior to the Pauline Letters. The Paul of the undisputed letters, however, is fond of verbs compounded with the preposition σύν (e.g., 1 Cor. 4:8; 12:26; Gal. 2:19; Phil. 3:10; 2 Cor. 7:3; Rom. 6:4, 6, 8; 8:17), and uses the verb ζωοποιέω to speak of the link between Christ's resurrection and the resurrection of believers (Rom. 8:11; cf. 1 Cor. 15:22; Best 1998: 214). He can also use the preposition σύν with the verb ζάω (zaō, live) either separately (1 Thess. 5:10) or in a compounded form (Rom. 6:8), to speak of Christians living with the resurrected Christ. The second σύν verb, συνεγείρω (*synegeirō*, raise together with), appears only here and in Colossians (2:12; 3:1) in the NT; yet again, the idea that the believer's resurrection from the dead is closely linked to Christ's resurrection is common coinage in early Christian literature and is especially characteristic of Paul."[15]

After drawing the obvious connection with Colossians 2:13, Thielman, like many other Biblical scholars, draws the connection between Paul's use of συζωοποιέω in Ephesians 2:5 with Baptism. But, disappointingly, he believes that because συνεζωοποίησεν is an aorist that the past tense nature of this verb and the two that follow may be indicative of possible shift in Paul's theology. Thielman asks:

> Is all this a sign that Ephesians comes from a time in which Paul's apocalyptic outlook (with its expectation of the resurrection and future salvation) has faded and now salvation is accomplished, albeit still by God's grace, through baptism into the church (Luz 1976: 369–75)? Does this passage show a decided retreat from the Pauline, and even Colossian, teaching on suffering with Christ, a retreat driven by the author's concern to see baptism as the union between the believer and Christ in his role as "head" (Hahn 2002: 363–64; cf. Berger 1995: 568–69)?[16]

The answer to both of Thielman's questions is no. Unfortunately, Thielman's view of the sacraments may be causing him to see Paul's use of the aorist with these verbs as a shift in his theology rather than a use that is consistent with the Biblical understanding of God's work in Baptism. Lenski, who confessed the Lutheran doctrine of baptism, does not see Paul's use of the aorist with συζωοποιέω as a shift in Paul's

---

[15] Thielman, 134.

[16] Ibid., 136.

theology but rather as being consistent with the mystical nature of baptism. Lenski states:

> Paul uses mystical language: "you" ("us") as dead "he quickened together with the Christ and raised up together and seated together." Mystical means neither mysterious nor mystic. Compare the other notable passage where Paul uses mystical terms, Rom. 6:4, etc. Here we have no figures, symbols, or verbal beauties but concentrated facts. One set of facts applies to the Christ physically, in his human nature; the other set applies to us spiritually. The two sets are drawn together into one. The interval of time is ignored. All are viewed as one, what God did with the Christ in the three acts and what he later did with us. Yet the difference remains. God vivified Christ in the tomb, raised him up from the dead, seated him at his right hand. God then did three similar spiritual things with us, the spiritual effects of what he did with the human nature of the Christ. The verbs compounded with σύν, "together," combine Christ and us in these acts. Cause and effect do go together; this σύν is a fact. Rom. 6:4, etc., states that this effect, namely making us alive with Christ, was mediated for us by baptism. That makes baptism the divine means of regeneration (John 3:3, 5)...
>
> Us God "quickened together with Christ." This expresses more than likeness: Christ physically dead and then physically quickened—we spiritually dead and then spiritually quickened. This is not allegory like physical leprosy—the leprosy of sin; physical blindness—spiritual blindness. "Together with the Christ" states a vital connection, that of cause and effect. Yet "together with" must not be stressed to mean that in the instant of Christ's physical vivification in the tomb all of us Christians were also spiritually vivified; the preposition in the verb is not that strong. The interval of time remains. The spiritual effect produced in us coincides with our baptism (Rom. 6:4, etc.).[17]

In verse six, Paul now continues with two more *together with* verbs, "and he (God) raised us up together with (συνεγείρω) (him) and seated us with (συγκαθίζω) (him) in the heavenlies, in Christ Jesus." Thielman notes that:

---

[17] Lenski, 415–417.

...although in their compounded form the verbs are unusual, the ideas conveyed by the compounded forms are not uncommon in the New Testament.

...The Paul of the undisputed letters, however, is fond of verbs compounded with the preposition σύν (e.g., 1 Cor. 4:8; 12:26; Gal. 2:19; Phil. 3:10; 2 Cor. 7:3; Rom. 6:4, 6, 8; 8:17), and uses the verb ζωοποιέω to speak of the link between Christ's resurrection and the resurrection of believers (Rom. 8:11; cf. 1 Cor. 15:22; Best 1998: 214). He can also use the preposition σύν with the verb ζάω (zaō, live) either separately (1 Thess. 5:10) or in a compounded form (Rom. 6:8), to speak of Christians living with the resurrected Christ. The second σύν verb, συνεγείρω (*synegeirō*, raise together with), appears only here and in Colossians (2:12; 3:1) in the NT; yet again, the idea that the believer's resurrection from the dead is closely linked to Christ's resurrection is common coinage in early Christian literature and is especially characteristic of Paul (1 Cor. 15:12–22, 48). The third term, συγκαθίζω (*synkathizo*, sit together with), appears only here in a transitive sense in the NT (cf. Luke 22:55), but the thought that the people of God will reign with God or Christ in heaven is not uncommon in literature from the period (Aune 1997: 261–62). The most unusual element about all three verbs is their past tense: here the Christian's life, resurrection, and royal position with Christ are *events that have already happened.*[18]

One has to wonder, in light of the fact that Paul is referencing Baptism, if the reason why he chose to use these three unusual verbs that speak to our being made alive with, being raised with, and seated with Christ, in rapid succession was in order to call to mind the Triune baptismal formula.

Verse 7 then reveals the purpose for all of this amazing grace; it is "in order that he (God) might demonstrate in the coming ages the surpassing riches of his grace in kindness toward us in Christ Jesus." F.F. Bruce explains that Paul is telling us in this verse that, "throughout time and in eternity the church, this society of pardoned rebels, is designed by God to be the masterpiece of his goodness."[19]

Pastorally, it is significant to note that Paul is writing these comforting gospel words as if the Ephesians *are already* Christians:

---

[18] Thielman, 134.
[19] Bruce, 288.

they have *already* been raised, united, and seated with Christ, they are *already* now saved. There isn't even the slightest hint to the contrary. To speak this way requires unflagging confidence in the promises of the Gospel and a boldness that is sadly lacking in far too many Lutheran pulpits. These verses challenge pastors to proclaim these same promises with the same boldness and confidence to the members of their congregation.

In those congregations where the pastor mixes and confuses law and gospel, people leave the church wondering if they're even saved. Law preaching can never boldly proclaim that a person is saved. Instead, law preaching always ends up saying, "work really hard to obey God and cross your fingers and hope that it's enough." But Paul here dares to announce and proclaim that the Christians reading this letter have had God's grace lavished on them. If one of the primary tasks of the pastoral office is to preach the word (and it is), then ought not pastors boldly give a living voice to these comforting gospel words with the same unyielding confidence that the Christians under their care are every bit as saved as the Ephesian Christians who first read this epistle?

This, not from yourselves...

Now comes the grand finale of this gospel fireworks extravaganza, and a sentence that has no equal in all of literature, "For by grace you have been saved through faith, and this not from yourselves, (it is) the gift of God, not from works, in order that no one might boast." Paul might as well have dropped the microphone and walked off stage. Every form of religious self-righteousness and every self-salvation scheme, whether pagan or manifesting within the visible church is defeated with this sentence. The perfect passive participle σεσῳσμένοι leaves no room for doubt. This verbal construction makes it clear that you are saved past tense and are being saved presently and the passive form makes it unmistakably clear that you're not doing the saving, God is.

Despite the fact that this sentence does not say that were saved by grace *alone* (*sola fide*) the words οὐκ ἐξ ἔργων categorically rule out any form of salvation by works. Said, Thielman, the statement οὐκ ἐξ ἔργων:

> ...denies that salvation comes "from" any "works" they might accomplish (ἐξ ἔργων, *ex ergōn*). Prior to their conversion, "the Ruler of the realm of the air" was powerfully at work (ἐνεργοῦντος, *energountos*) in them, and they followed the

cravings of their fallen flesh and mind (vv. 2–3). Accomplishing their own salvation, therefore, was impossible.[20]

When reading Luther's explanation of the 3rd Article of the Creed in the Small Catechism in light of this entire portion of Ephesians but particularly in light of this sentence it becomes evident that the words of this verse sunk deep into Luther's heart and theology:

> I believe that by my own reason or strength I cannot believe in Jesus Christ, my Lord, or come to him. But the Holy Spirit has called me through the Gospel, enlightened me with his gifts, and sanctified and preserved me in true faith, just as he calls, gathers, enlightens, and sanctifies the whole Christian church on earth and preserves it in union with Jesus Christ in the one true faith.[21]

One could argue convincingly that this portion of the Small Catechism is a succinct summary and restating of Paul's words from Ephesians 2:4-9. Is it any wonder why Luther so strongly proclaimed and defended *Sola Fide*?

Now that Paul has definitively laid out the fact that salvation from beginning to end is God's work, he explains the role of good works and what he reveals is not an afterthought. It is an explosive revelation about the new reality we live in and how that impacts the conduct of our lives. Paul explains, "[F]or we are his creation, created in Christ Jesus for good works which God prepared beforehand that we might conduct our lives in them." In the opening verses of this chapter Paul described our state as dead in trespasses "in which you conducted your life" (περιπατέω) and now Paul reintroduces the word περιπατέω to bookend his thoughts and the idea is explosively simple. Paul is saying, you formerly conducted your lives in the same way as those who are dead in trespasses and sins naturally conduct their lives i.e. according to this age of the world, according to the ruler of the power of the air, in the desires of our flesh, doing the will of the flesh and the mind. But, now that God has made you alive together with Christ, you are His creation (a new creation) and now we conduct our lives as those who are alive i.e. doing the good works which God has prepared in advance for us to do. In other words, dead people conduct their lives as dead people, and living people conduct their lives as living people. The

---

[20] Thielman, 143.
[21] Tappert, 345.

eschatological reality of the new creation has already broken forth. We are already a part of it, and it changes everything. Thielman writes:

> The idea that Christians are part of a new, eschatological creation appears in the undisputed letters (Gal. 6:15; 2 Cor. 5:17) and plays a role in the ethical admonitions in Colossians (3:10), where the theme of Christ as the agent of the original creation is prominent (1:15, 23). In Ephesians too, Christ is the agent of the new creation (2:15b), and the idea of a new creation lays the groundwork for some of the letter's ethical admonitions in its second section (4:13, 22, 24).[22]

F.F. Bruce puts it this way:

> The work of grace which has transformed those who were spiritually and morally dead into new men and women, alive with the resurrection life of Christ, is God's work from first to last: "we are his workmanship." The word so translated is used in one other place in the Pauline writings—in Rom. 1:20, where it refers (in the plural) to God's created works. Here, however, it refers to the new creation of which Paul speaks more than once. This new creation (as is emphasized below in v. 15) transcends natural distinctions of the old order: in it "neither circumcision counts for anything, nor uncircumcision, but a new creation" (Gal. 6:15); "if anyone is in Christ, there is a new creation; the old has passed away, behold, the new has come" (2 Cor. 5:17). The new heaven and earth of which an OT prophet spoke (Isa. 65:17; 66:22) have come into existence already in this new order, "created in Christ Jesus." If those who belonged to the old order were dead through their trespasses and sins, those who belong to the new creation are characterized by "good works," *works performed not to secure salvation but as the fruit of salvation.*[23]

This passage clearly and unambiguously omits works from our justification and then puts works in their proper place. It is so clear and decisive that Thielman and F.F. Bruce after carefully exegeting this passage sound like exactly like the Lutheran reformers in their understanding of good works as it relates to justification. Here is how

---

[22] Thielman, 145.
[23] Bruce, 290–291.

the Epitome of the Formula of Concord affirmatively teaches good works and the nature of their necessity:

> **1.** That good works, like fruits of a good tree, certainly and indubitably follow genuine faith—if it is a living and not a dead faith.
>
> **2.** We believe, teach, and confess that good works should be completely excluded from a discussion of the article of man's salvation as well as from the article of our justification before God. The Apostle affirms in clear terms, "So also David declares that salvation pertains only to the man to whom God reckons righteousness apart from works, saying, 'Blessed are those whose iniquities are forgiven, and whose sins are covered'" (Rom. 4:6–8). And again, "For by grace you have been saved through faith; and this is not your own doing, it is the gift of God—not because of works, lest any man should boast" (Eph. 2:8–9).
>
> **3.** We believe, teach, and confess further that all men, but especially those who are regenerated and renewed by the Holy Spirit, are obligated to do good works.
>
> **4.** In this sense the words "necessary," "ought," and "must" are correctly and in a Christian way applied to the regenerated and are in no way contrary to the pattern of sound words and terminology.
>
> **5.** However, when applied to the regenerated the words "necessity" and "necessary" are to be understood as involving not coercion but the due obedience which genuine believers, in so far as they are reborn, render not by coercion or compulsion of the law but from a spontaneous spirit because they are "no longer under the law but under grace."[24]

By checking what the Lutheran reformers wrote about good works against this passage of scripture we are able to see that they understood this text perfectly. They got it right.

This has vast pastoral implications. This passage of scripture solves the puzzle and reveals how we as Christians—those who have been raised by God, united, and seated with Christ in our baptisms, and have been saved by God's grace as a free gift—are to understand the role of good works. Instead of doing these works to earn God's favor and earn our salvation, we do them *because* we are a new creation,

---

[24] Tappert,, 476–477.

because God made us alive. We are no longer dead in trespasses and sins; therefore it would be foolish to conduct our lives as those who are dead. Instead, we can embrace the good works that God has prepared for us to do because He has made us alive. There is no room in this passage for the idea that we do good works in order to be made alive. Paul, is in a very real sense, saying that you are no longer dead, you have been made alive, therefore live and conduct your life in the good works God has prepared for those whom He has raised. It's glorious! It gives us a way to do good works in freedom, joy and excitement rather than in fear or in order to merit eternal life. This is what the people in our congregations need to hear and understand.

Summary

It would not be an overstatement to say that Ephesians 2:1-10 is the most important passage of all of scripture. It gives us the keys to rightly understanding the doctrines of Original Sin and Justification by Grace Through Faith and then gives us the keys to rightly understanding the role and function of good works in the lives of Christians. The person who rightly understands this portion of scripture will by necessity also rightly understand all of scripture. The person who is ignorant of or misunderstands this text will never be able to understand the Bible and the comforting message that it contains about the God who is rich in grace and mercy who saves us, not because of works done by us, but by grace through faith alone.

Bibligography

Kurt Aland et al., *Novum Testamentum Graece*, 28th Edition. (Stuttgart: Deutsche Bibelgesellschaft, 2012.)

Walter Bauer, William Arndt, Frederick W. Danker, and William Gingrich, *A Greek-English Lexicon of the New Testament and Other Early Christian Literature*. (Chicago: University of Chicago Press, 2000.)

F. F. Bruce, *The Epistles to the Colossians, to Philemon, and to the Ephesians*, The New International Commentary on the New Testament. (Grand Rapids, MI: Wm. B. Eerdmans Publishing Co., 1984.)

R. C. H. Lenski, *The Interpretation of St. Paul's Epistles to the Galatians, to the Ephesians and to the Philippians* (Columbus, O.: Lutheran Book Concern, 1937.)

Andrew T. Lincoln, *Ephesians*, vol. 42, Word Biblical Commentary. (Dallas: Word, Incorporated, 1990.)

Francis Pieper, *Christian Dogmatics*, electronic ed., vol. 1. (St. Louis: Concordia Publishing House, 1953.)

Theodore G. Tappert, ed., *The Book of Concord the Confessions of the Evangelical Lutheran Church*. (Philadelphia: Mühlenberg Press, 1959.)

Frank Thielman, *Ephesians*, Baker Exegetical Commentary on the New Testament (Grand Rapids, MI: Baker Academic, 2010.)

Obedientia Christi Activa: The Imputation of Christ's Active Obedience in the Lutheran Tradition and Scripture

By Jordan Cooper

The doctrine of justification that comes to us by grace alone through faith alone on account of Christ alone has been labeled the *articulus stantis et cadentis ecclesiae*—the article upon which the church stands or falls—in the Lutheran tradition. Yet, though there is agreement as to the centrality of this doctrine, controversies surrounding the nature of justification have not ceased in the Lutheran church. Soon after the death of Luther, Osiander proposed that justification was the result of Christ's indwelling divine nature, rather than an act of forensic imputation. This resulted in a fierce debate which was concluded by the Formula of Concord, but the issue of justification was far from settled; other controversies have arisen since the publication of the Book of Concord in 1580.

In recent decades, one of the main facets of the historic teaching of justification that has been challenged, is the doctrine of the imputation of Christ's active obedience. This is the belief that the righteousness merited by Christ for his people consists in his passive obedience, or his paying the penalty for sin on the cross, as well as his active obedience which consists in his fulfilling the law in order to gain righteousness which is imputed through faith. Though perhaps not explicitly stated in the writings of Martin Luther himself on this subject, the imputation of Christ's active obedience is confessed in the Formula of Concord:

> Therefore, his obedience consists not only in his suffering and death but also in the fact that he freely put himself in our place under the law and fulfilled the law with this obedience and reckoned it to us as righteousness. As a result of his total obedience—which he performed on our behalf for God in his deeds and suffering, in life and death—God forgives our sin, considers us upright and righteous, and grants us eternal salvation. (FC SD.15)

Though no extensive debate existed on this issue during the sixteenth century, the Brandenburg theologian George Karg rejected the imputation of Christ's active obedience.[1] He argued that since obedience to law is an obligation for God's creatures, one could not gain merit through such obedience.[2] The Formula settled the question for the immediate years following the Reformation, yet it has been under extensive scrutiny since the nineteenth century.

Theologians of disparate perspectives have rejected the doctrine of the imputation of Christ's active obedience in recent years. Modernist theologians in the late nineteenth and early twentieth centuries tended to reject the doctrine of Christ's active obedience for moral reasons.[3] It was said that the moral character of the gospel was lost through a reliance on Christ's own holiness as imputed to humanity. One of the prominent opponents of the imputation of Christ's active obedience are the proponents of the so-called "New Perspective on Paul," most significantly N.T. Wright. In this view, the imputation of Christ's active obedience as a doctrine was developed through reading medieval debates about merit into the text of the Pauline epistles. This doctrine is not explicitly taught in Paul, nor was it something that was an aspect of his Jewish worldview. From a Reformed point of view, there are certain proponents of the Federal Vision movement who have rejected the imputation of Christ's active obedience on the basis of a modified covenant theology, often referred to as Monocovenantalism.[4] These writers view the active obedience of Christ as necessary for Jesus to be qualified as the spotless lamb to die on the cross, but is not imputed to his people per say. Also, the notion of merit in any sense, whether the merit of the Christian or of Christ himself, is problematic for these writers. In Baptist theology, some in the "New Covenant Theology" movement have also rejected the doctrine of active obedience due to their emphasis on the discontinuity of the covenants. In this perspective, the law is invalid for the new

---

[1] Karg retracted this belief after being removed from his teaching position and was consequently reinstated.

[2] This same argument was put forward by Anselm in *Cur Deus Homo?*

[3] This is reflected for example in Harnack's treatise "What is Christianity?," wherein he argues that the religion of Paul as misinterpreted by the Reformers, lost the moral center of Jesus' own gospel (which is about God the Father) for a gospel about Jesus. Harnack argues, in contrast to the Reformers, that central tenants of Christianity are the Fatherhood of God and the brotherhood of man.

[4] See for example, Norman Shepherd's article, "The Imputation of Christ's Active Obedience," in *Sandlin, Andrew P. A Faith That is Never Alone: A Response to Westminster Seminary California.* La Grange, CA: Kerygma, 2007, 249-278.

covenant member, thus there is no need for Christ to fulfill the law on behalf of believers.

The rejection of the doctrine of active obedience in contemporary Lutheranism is perhaps most central for this paper. For those who adopt a *Quia* subscription to the confessional documents, this issue is settled due to its presence in the Formula of Concord. However, theologians of other Lutheran traditions, who do not accept the authority of the Formula of Concord, have deviated from this teaching. One influential theologian who has done this is Gerhard O. Forde. Forde's career was centered on the doctrine of justification by faith as perceived it in the writings of the early Luther. He argues that justification by faith alone must once again become the central doctrine of Lutheranism, and be boldly proclaimed from Lutheran pulpits. Forde does not, however, adopt the traditional scholastic approach to justification, but proposes a view which he argues is consistent with Luther's own theology as opposed to the later Confessional documents.

Gerhard Forde's View of Justification

Gerhard Forde's doctrine of justification is articulated in contrast to traditional approaches to imputation in his book *Where God Meets Man*. Forde argues, in this volume, that all theology has tended to adopt either a ladder scheme of salvation, or an eschatological approach to justification. He rejects the former in favor of the latter. The ladder scheme is a theology of merit. In Forde's view, this characterizes both Roman Catholic theology and Protestant scholastic teaching. For both, there is a ladder to heaven that is characterized by one's merit or obedience to the law. In the Roman Catholic scheme, this ladder is climbed through the merit of Christ, the saints, and one's own good works. The Protestants have unfortunately adopted a similar system:

> We begin by assuming the law is a ladder to heaven. Then we go on to say, "Of course, no one can climb the ladder, because we are all weakened by sin. We are therefore guilty and lost." And this is where "the gospel" is to enter the picture. What we need is someone to pay our debt to God and to climb the ladder for us. This, supposedly, is what Jesus has done. As our "substitute" he has paid of God and climbed the ladder for us. All we have to do is "believe" it.[5]

------

[5] Gerhard Forde. *Where God Meets Man*. (Minneapolis: Augsburg, 1972), 10.

In this perspective, one cannot affirm either substitutionary atonement, or the imputation of Christ's active obedience. Both of these doctrines, which developed through the work of Melanchthon and Chemnitz, do not depart significantly from the Roman Catholic soteriological paradigm, because they both depend on the conviction that the law needs to be fulfilled for God's justice to be satisfied. This destroys the eschatological nature of the gospel which breaks free from the constraints of God's law. He purports:

> We have, in fact, interpreted the gospel merely as something that makes the ladder scheme work. The gospel comes to make up for the deficiencies of the law. The gospel does not come as anything really new. It is not the breaking in of a radically new age with an entirely new outlook. It is simply a "repair job." It merely fixes up the old where it had broken down. It is an attempt to put new wine in old wine skins, or a new patch on an old garment. When we do this, the gospel always comes off as second best. It is trapped in the understanding of law which we have ourselves concocted.[6]

When arguing for such a view of the gospel, where Christ dies as a substitute for one's failure to obey the law, and lives righteously under the law in order that his obedience might be imputed to his people: "The gospel itself simply becomes another kind of law."[7]

Forde argues that this destroys the nature of forgiveness. He asks: "If God has been paid, how can one say that he really forgives? If a debt is paid, one can hardly say it is forgiven. Nor could one call God's action mercy."[8] He assumes that God's justice should not and does not require payment for sin, because forgiveness has to be given without conditions. The law is based on conditions, but the gospel is free and unbound to law. An important aspect of Forde's scheme of law is the manner in which the term "law" is defined. For Forde, "The law is not defined only as a specific set of demands as such, but rather in terms of what it does to you."[9] Rather than speaking of law as Torah, a specific set of commands that adhere to God's moral nature, Forde opts for an existential understanding of the law. The law, as well as the gospel, is not defined by its content, but its effect on the hearer. He argues that, "The gospel too, is defined primarily by what it does: the

---

[6] Ibid., 11.
[7] Ibid., 11.
[8] Ibid., 12.
[9] Ibid., 15.

gospel comforts because it puts an end to the voice of the law."[10] Theological attempts to define the gospel by Christ's active and passive obedience are what Forde labels "spectator theology." They depend on an assumption that the gospel is a theory with a set of truths that one must adhere to, rather than the doing of God. He argues:

> When it [a theology of glory] is applied to the event of the cross itself, this kind of thinking leads back to the theology of the ladder. The law is the way of salvation, a ladder to heaven. Because we have failed and are too weak to climb it, Jesus becomes our substitute. By his perfect life he climbs the ladder and by his death he pays for our failure. In terms of dogmatic theology, Jesus "vicariously satisfied" the demands of the law. He paid the bill, so to speak, which we couldn't pay. Such theology is a spectator theology. It is the result of an attempt to fit the cross into a system of meaning which one already has and which remains standing as an eternal scheme indicating what would have to be done to placate God.[11]

The ideas of both substitutionary atonement and the imputation of active obedience are dependent upon a theology of glory, rather than a theology of the cross. This harkens back to Luther's Heidelberg Disputation of 1515 which is highly influential for Forde's own theology. Interestingly, Forde does admit that Luther did "use language which sounds like vicarious satisfaction language,"[12] but then makes the statement that, "Luther vehemently rejects the idea that God is one who can be bargained with in commercial fashion or satisfied in the sense that amends may be made to him."[13] Forde gives no citations from Luther to defend this statement; it needs to be substantiated that Luther would reject substitution when he himself utilized such language.

Rather than substitution, or the imputation of merit, Forde purports that justification is primarily to be defined as a death and resurrection. He states that, "'Full and complete justification' is equated with death and resurrection, not with a legal scheme as such."[14] Again, in another place, Forde argues that justification "means precisely not some sort of legal transaction but, according to the New Testament, a

---

[10] Ibid., 16.

[11] Ibid., 34.

[12] Ibid., 41.

[13] Ibid., 41-42.

[14] Gerhard Forde. *Justification by Faith: A Matter of Life and Death* (Mifflintown, PA: Sigler, 1991), 16.

death and a resurrection."[15] Forde does admit that one can, in some sense, talk about justification as forensic and legal. He purports that, "Righteousness comes just by divine pronouncement, by divine 'imputation' as Luther liked to put it."[16] Justification is "a re-creative act of God, something he does precisely by speaking unconditionally."[17] Forde certainly is willing to speak of imputation. God imputes the sinner righteous by faith, but that is not by the imputation of Christ's merit to the sinner. It is rather a free forensic declaration that creates new life, so that "justification and death-life are complimentary."[18] He even argues that, "The more forensic it is the more effective it is!"[19]

Biblical Evidence

Although Forde's argument against the imputation of Christ's active obedience rests largely upon historical arguments from Luther's writings, the primary source in defining doctrine should be Scripture rather than Luther's own theology. The Lutheran church does not subscribe to Luther's own theology as its primary theological statement. Rather, as heir of the Reformation, the church adopts the *sola scriptura* principle, and the Lutheran Confessional documents as correct interpretations of holy writ.

In my previous study of Luther, I have not found convincing evidence that Luther did indeed adopt the concept of the imputation of Christ's obedience under the law.[20] Luther seems to connect Christ's righteousness largely with his death and resurrection rather than his active obedience per say. That, however, does not necessitate a rejection of the concept.

Although Forde is correct to emphasize the language of death and resurrection in justification, and properly asserts that salvation should not be limited to strictly legal metaphors, it is apparent through biblical study that the historical formulation of Christ's active and passive obedience is a necessary and beneficial discussion. It is true that the Lutheran scholastics often over-emphasized the centrality of Christ's active obedience in justification while neglecting the centrality of the resurrection in God's justifying act. It is also true that they tended to place vicarious satisfaction in a more central role than did

---

[15] Ibid., 10.

[16] Ibid., 29.

[17] Ibid., 30.

[18] Ibid., 36.

[19] Ibid., 36.

[20] I discuss this in: Jordan Cooper. *The Righteousness of One: An Evaluation of Early Patristic Soteriology in Light of the New Perspective on Paul.* (Eugene, OR: Wipf & Stock, 2013), 40-67.

Luther or Paul, who emphasized a *Christus Victor* approach to the atonement. They were not, however, wrong in teaching these doctrines (though this paper focuses on the active obedience aspect of justification rather than the theology of vicarious atonement) simply because their emphasis may have been off balance. It will be demonstrated that though many of the arguments that have been traditionally used to defend this idea are unconvincing, there is ample ground for such an idea in the biblical text.

Romans 5

Much of the exegetical discussion regarding Christ's active obedience centers on Paul's contrast between Adam and Christ in Romans 5. Brian Vickers, in fact, claims that: "It is not an exaggeration to say that the imputation of Christ's righteousness hangs on the interpretation of Romans 5:12-21."[21] Of particular debate is the following section:

> And the free gift is not like the result of that one man's sin. For the judgment following one trespass brought condemnation, but the free gift following many trespasses brought justification. For if, because of one man's trespass, death reigned through that one man, much more will those who receive the abundance of grace and the free gift of righteousness reign in life through the one man Jesus Christ. Therefore, as one trespass led to condemnation for all men, so one act of righteousness leads to justification and life for all men. For as by the one man's disobedience the many were made sinners, so by the one man's obedience the many will be made righteous. (Rom. 5:16-19)

In this text, Paul contrasts the work of Adam in the garden, and the work of Christ. Something that Adam did brought condemnation and the making of sinners, and some act of obedience on the part of Christ resulted in many being made righteous. What needs to be determined is what "one act" Paul refers to in this text.

Reformed theologian David VanDrunen gives a classic Calvinistic exposition of this text in defense of active obedience in his essay, "To Obey is Better than Sacrifice."[22] VanDrunen explains that his

---

[21] Brian Vickers. *Jesus' Blood and Righteousness: Paul's Theology of Imputation.* (Wheaton: Crossway, 2006), 199.

[22] David VanDrunen. "To Obey is Better Than Sacrifice," in Johnson L., Gary and Guy P. Waters. *By Faith Alone: Answering the Challenges to the Doctrine of Justification.* (Wheaton: Crossway, 2006), 127-146.

exposition of this text is rooted in his understanding of covenant theology. In traditional Reformed covenant theology, a distinction is made between the covenant of grace and the covenant of works.[23] The covenant of works is a covenant with conditions. God gives blessings based on merit. The Adamic administration is an instance of the covenant of works, wherein God promised Adam life based on his obedience. There was no grace in this covenant, only merit and reward. Adam served as a federal head of the human race, being representative of the entirety of humanity. The first man was placed in a probationary period in the covenant of works. If he obeyed the law, Adam would be confirmed in righteousness, and the future human race alone with him; if he disobeyed, he would be punished with physical and spiritual death, and his descendants would be imputed as guilty and born in sin due to the act of their representative. In this scheme, Christ, as the second Adam, was also placed into the covenant of works. Like Adam, Christ was required to obey the law perfectly so that those whom he represented (the elect) would be imputed righteous. In this scheme, there is both an alien guilt (Adam) and an alien righteousness (Christ's). It is this parallel between Adam and Christ in the covenant of works that then frames the doctrine of active obedience. White and Beisner argue:

> [T]he relationship of Adam's seed (the whole human race naturally born) to God in the covenant of works was like the redemption of Christ's seed (the elect) to God in the covenants of redemption and grace. For both Adam's seed and Christ's seed, the inheritance of eternal life is conditioned on the obedience of their representative and is, therefore, procured vicariously for the seed by the meritorious works of another. The crucial difference between the two seeds is, of course, that Adam failed to fulfill the condition for his seed and thus failed, as their representative, to merit eternal life for them, while Christ fulfilled the covenantal condition for his seed and thus did, as their representative, merit eternal life for them and pay

---

[23] For a brief exposition of this theological approach see: Michael S. Horton, "Covenant and Justification: Engaging N.T. Wright and John Piper," in *Justified: Modern Reformation Essays on the Doctrine of Justification.* (Escondido: Modern Reformation, 2010) , 11-32. For a more detailed look at this view, see: Michael S. Horton, *Introducing Covenant Theology.* (Grand Rapids: Baker, 2009).

the penalty for which they were liable due to Adam's (and their own) demerit.[24]

Since the Adamic administration is primarily one of merit, then the actions of Christ are defined primarily in merit categories, which is why Reformed theology has often placed Christ's active obedience in a much more central role than Lutherans have.

It is in this context that VanDrunen exposits Romans 5. He argues that, "Paul's concern in this pericope is with justification and the covenant of works."[25] In the beginning of the above text in Paul, starting in verse 16, Paul contrasts righteousness and condemnation. This, for VanDrunen, is necessarily covenantal because "the references to Adam, transgression, the disobedience of the one, and death draws readers to the covenant of works at creation."[26] Because verse 17 begins with γάρ (for), VanDrunen argues that, "Verse 17 explains what the justification mentioned in 5:16 entails."[27] In other words, justification involves the granting of the "free gift of righteousness." It is this free gift of righteousness which is then connected to the obedience of Christ in contrast to Adam. VanDrunen summarizes: "Paul asserts that a gift brings justification (5:16), this gift is a gift of righteousness (5:17), this gift of righteousness focuses upon one righteous act (5:18), and this righteous act is the obedience of the one man, Jesus Christ (5:19)."[28]

The problem faced by VanDrunen and other proponents of active obedience as a referent in this passage is with the phrase ἑνὸς δικαιώματος (one act of righteousness). The contrast made by Paul is not between Adam's entire life of obedience and Christ's entire life of obedience, but between one act of Adam and one act of Christ. VanDrunen offers a number of counterarguments in defense of one act of righteousness being a referent to Christ's entire life of obedience. He first counters the argument that the phrase "one act" cannot refer to multiple acts with the question: "Was the crucifixion really one act of Christ? Insofar as Christ submitted himself to this fate and interacted with his Father and those around him, the crucifixion itself was a series of actions rather than a single act."[29] In VanDrunen's view, if this text references either Christ's active or passive obedience, it has to be referencing multiple acts rather than a single one.

---

[24] R. Fowler White, and E. Calvin Beisner, "Covenant, Inheritance, and Typology," in *By Faith Alone*, 154-155.
[25] Van Drunen, *To Obey is Better than Sacrifice*, 142.
[26] Ibid., 142.
[27] Ibid., 142.
[28] Ibid., 143.
[29] Ibid., 143.

This argument remains unconvincing for a number of reasons. First, any action can be divided up into several acts. For example, when Adam ate of the tree, he first had to listen to Eve, and then he thought about the act before he performed it, he moved has hand toward the fruit, he put the fruit in his mouth, he bit and chewed it, and he also swallowed it. Just because one act can be divided in a certain manner of thinking into several different actions does not mean that speaking of "one act" is an elastic concept that can refer to any length of time or number of actions. In the same manner that Adam's act of eating the forbidden fruit can be said to be a single action, so can the crucifixion when viewed broadly. It is a common manner of speaking to associate a number of actions performed toward the same end in a finite period of time as "one act." For example, it would be common for one to refer to the September 11th terrorist attacks which devastated the United States as a horrible singular act of violence, even though the action involved a number of different steps. If one were to speak of one terrible act that the terrorists responsible performed, would anyone assume that this could be a reference to all of the evil actions that these evil figures performed, including their education, training, and previous acts of violence? It is common parlance to refer to a number of connected actions within a short time span which are performed toward a common end as one act, but not every action performed by an individual for thirty three years. Unless some precedent for understanding multiple years-worth of actions as a single event can be found in other literature, this is not a tenable argument.

The second problem with this argument is that the parallel does not fit. Unless one has a preconceived covenant of works/covenant of grace grid through which this text is understood, there is no parallel between one act of disobedience on the part of Adam, and thousands of actions of obedience performed by Christ. The parallel Paul makes is between ἑνὸς δικαιώματος (one act of righteousness) and ἑνὸς παραπτώματος (one trespass). If one action of Adam is being discussed here, then so is one action of Christ. This is how this was understood in the Patristic period. John Chrysostom, for example, when discussing Romans 5 states:

> Now this is why Adam is a type of Christ. How a type? it will be said. Why in that, as the former became to those who were sprung from him, although they had not eaten of the tree, the cause of that death which by his eating was introduced; thus also did Christ become to those who sprung from Him, even though they had not wrought righteousness, the Provider of

that righteousness which is through His Cross He graciously bestowed on us all.[30]

Chrysostom speaks here of righteousness that is bestowed, which is provided by Christ, but he connects it not with Christ's active obedience, but with his death on the cross. This is similar to how Irenaeus interprets this passage. Though Irenaeus emphasized the importance of Christ's righteous life in other contexts, he does not connect this to Romans 5. Instead, he writes that, "As by means of a tree we were made debtors to God, [so also] by means of a tree we may obtain the remission of our debt."[31] Prior to the development of Protestant scholastic categories, Pauline interpreters did not view Romans 5 as a reference to Christ's obedient life.

Finally, there are references to Christ's redemptive work in the immediate context, but none of those references refer to his obedience to the law. In verse 9 of chapter 5, Paul connects righteousness specifically with Christ's death. He argues: "Now, having been justified by his blood (δικαιωθέντες νὺν ἐν τῶ αἵματι αὐτοῦ σωθησόμεθα) we will be saved by the wrath of God through him." He then continues his argument, writing, "For if while we were enemies we were reconciled to God by the death of his Son, much more, now that we are reconciled, shall we be saved by his life" (Rom. 5:9-10). Paul parallels the concept of reconciliation (καταλλαγέντες) and justification (δικαιωθέντες), and attributes both to the death of Christ. Paul then references Christ's life of mediation as the means by which final salvation will be received (5:11). The discussion of Christ as the second Adam begins in verse 12, and is not a separate discussion as is demonstrated by the use of Διά τοῦτο (therefore), prior to describing the effects of sin. The only conceivable way in which these two discussions can be connected is if the righteous act of Jesus in verse 19 is connected with his righteous act of verses 9 and 10 which is his death on the cross, not his obedience to the law.

Reading the Justification Texts Synoptically
It may seem that since Romans 5 does not teach the imputation of Christ's active obedience, which Vickers calls "the best ground for asserting that Christ's righteousness, his positive obedience, is imputed

---

[30] Chrysostom, "The Epistle to the Romans," X.13., *Nicene and Post Nicene Fathers, First Series, Vol. 11*, (Peabody: Hendrickson, 2004), 402.
[31] Irenaeus, "Against Heresies," *Book V. XVII.3., Ante Nicene Fathers, Vol. 1.* (Peabody: Hendrickson, 2004), 545.

to believers,"[32] then there no longer remains any valid theological or exegetical reason to adopt the conviction that Christ's active obedience to the law is imputed to believers. However, though the text often used to defend the concept of active obedience does not teach such a concept, this idea is still valid based on several Biblical principles. First, it is to be noted that Paul continuously speaks of a righteousness being counted to the believer by faith. Brian Vickers helpfully demonstrates that the texts speaking of imputation need to be read synoptically. In other words, though no one texts explicitly states that through faith Christ's righteousness is imputed, this is clearly a Pauline concept when the various justification texts are read together.

First, there are several texts that speak of a righteousness that comes "from God." In Romans 3, for example, Paul speaks of "the righteousness of God has been manifested apart from the law, although the Law and the Prophets bear witness to it—the righteousness of God through faith in Jesus Christ for all who believe" (Rom. 3:21-22). This is a righteousness that belongs to God, but is given ἐις πάντας τούς πιστεύντας (to all who believe). In this text, Paul deals with the thesis statement of his epistle, expressed in chapter 1: "For I am not ashamed of the gospel, for it is the power of God for salvation to everyone who believes, to the Jew first and also to the Greek. For in it the righteousness of God is revealed from faith for faith, as it is written, 'The righteous shall live by faith'" (Rom. 1:16-17). In Paul's second epistle to the Corinthians, Paul again references the righteousness of God as something given to believers: "For our sake he made him to be sin who knew no sin, so that in him we might become the righteousness of God" (2 Cor. 5:21). In these texts it becomes apparent that there is a righteousness of God that believers somehow receive.

The second set of texts reference the imputation of righteousness through faith. Speaking of Abraham's faith, Paul writes: "And to the one who does not work but believes in him who justifies the ungodly, his faith is counted as righteousness" (Rom. 4:5). There are similar texts in Gal. 3:6, Rom. 4:9, and Rom. 4:22-24. Some interpreters, such as Robert Gundry, argue that Romans 4 teaches that faith is counted as righteous, not because it receives Christ's righteousness, but because faith, though not a work, is itself counted as righteousness. He argues that: "none of these texts say that Christ's righteousness was counted. With the exception of Romans 4:6...they say that Abraham's faith is counted, so that righteousness comes into view not as what is

---

[32] Vicars, 227.

counted but as what God counts faith to be."[33] This argument hinges upon the language of imputing (λογίζεται) faith for (εἰς) righteousness. The language of these particular texts cannot be used definitively to argue that faith itself is regarded as righteous, because as D.A. Carson demonstrates, there is grammatical precedent for something to be "imputed or reckoned as something else."[34] The problem with Gundry's argument is that he attempts to make his case from one particular grammatical construction instead of reading these verses within the context of Paul's overall theology.

The final set of texts that need to be examined in Paul's theology are those which connected the righteousness of God with Christ. In Philippians Paul writes:

> For his sake I have suffered the loss of all things and count them as rubbish, in order that I may gain Christ and be found in him, not having a righteousness of my own that comes from the law, but that which comes through faith in Christ, the righteousness from God that depends on faith. (Phil. 3:8-9)

What is important about this text is that Paul connects receiving the righteousness of God with being ἐν αὐτῷ (in him [Christ]), and is also with his desire that Χριστόν κερδήσω (I may gain Christ). He reiterates the same point in 2 Corinthians 5:21: "For our sake he made him to be sin who knew no sin, so that in him we might become the righteousness of God."[35] Again, it is only "in Christ" that one becomes the righteousness of God. There is one text where Paul specifically connects saving righteousness with that of Christ. In 1 Corinthians Paul writes that Christ "became to us wisdom from God, righteousness and sanctification and redemption" (2 Cor. 5:21). When read together, these three texts produce the inevitable conclusion that:

1. A righteousness is delivered from God for salvation.
2. Faith is credited, or imputed, as righteousness.
3. God's righteousness is only received "in Christ," and is one place identified with Christ explicitly.

---

[33] Robert H Gundry, "The Nonimputation of Christ's Righteousness," in Mark Husbands, and Daniel J. Treier. *Justification: What's at Stake in the Current Debates?* Downers Grove, IL: IVP, 2004, 18.

[34] D.A. Carson, "The Vindication of Imputation," *Justification: What's at Stake in the Current Debates?*, 58.

[35] emphasis added.

When these verses are harmonized, it becomes clear that through faith, the one who believes receives the righteousness of Christ as a gift. Now that this has been established, the question remains as to the content of this righteousness. If Romans 5 is taken as the sole text that expounds upon the nature of Christ's imputed righteousness, then it is clear that Christ's righteousness refers only to his death. However, other broader theological considerations make it apparent that this also has reference to Christ's fulfillment of the law.

A Biblical-Theological Approach to Active Obedience

The work of Christ needs to be approached in its broader theological context. The manner in which this should be done is not by imposing a "covenant of works/covenant of grace" scheme upon the Biblical text, but by using categories clearly defined and expounded in Scripture. Norman Shepherd argues that the broader Biblical context of Christ's threefold office is incommensurate with the doctrine of Christ's active obedience. Shepherd writes:

> The Old Testament prepares us for understanding the threefold office of Christ as prophet, priest and king in the work of the prophets, the priests, and the kings of the old economy. Throughout his public ministry Jesus served as a prophet announcing the coming of the kingdom of God and calling sinners to repentance. At the end of his ministry he offered himself as priest on the cross as a sacrifice for the sins of his people. After his resurrection he ascended into heaven to rule as king over his people and to build his church. In performing a lifetime of perfect and personal obedience, Christ is not doing the kind of official work assigned to prophets, priests, or kings as described in the Old Testament. However, in giving his life as a sacrifice for sin (passive obedience), Jesus is clearly doing the work of a priest as the Book of Hebrews makes abundantly obvious. The imputation of active obedience does not correlate with the way Scripture presents Christ to us as our prophet, priest, and king.[36]

The problem with Shepherd's proposal is that he negates what is perhaps the primary typological category of the Old Testament, that Christ does not only fulfill the threefold offices given to Israel, but that Jesus *is Israel itself.* If it is understood that Jesus does, in fact, fulfill the

---

[36] Shepherd, 266-267.

role of Israel, then there is ample place for Christ as the faithful Son who obeys on behalf of his people.

Two points, then, need to be substantiated for it to be proven that Jesus, as Israel, needed to be faithful to God's law in order that eternal life might be given to his people. First, it needs to be proven that Jesus is the fulfillment and embodiment of Israel. Second, it needs to be shown that Israel was required to keep the law in order to be given the Abrahamic blessings. The first point can be shown in a number of texts. Tremper Longman argues that the pattern of Jesus' life follows that of Israel. He states: "As the embodiment of the faithful remnant, he would undergo divine judgment for sin (on the cross), endure an exile (three days forsaken by God in the grave), and experience a restoration (resurrection) to life as the foundation of a new Israel, inheriting the promises of God afresh."[37] It is to be remembered that there was no idea in the Jewish faith that a messiah would be resurrected from the dead, but that Israel would experience resurrection at once. In rising from the dead alone, Jesus showed himself as the fulfillment of the hopes for a restoration of Israel.

Matthew's Gospel is particularly insightful on this point. David Scaer demonstrates that Matthew's Gospel is divided into five discourses, mirroring the five books of the Torah.[38] Jesus portrays himself as a new and better Moses by delivering the law on a mountain through the Sermon on the Mount. This is also apparent in the utilization of texts about Israel in reference to Jesus. Matthew cites the prophet Hosea as a reference to Christ's birth, writing: "This was to fulfill what the Lord had spoken by the prophet, 'Out of Egypt I called my son'" (Matt. 2:15). If one examines the text in Hosea, it is apparent that this verse references the nation of Israel. The full verse states: "When Israel was a child, I loved him, and out of Egypt I called my son" (Hosea 11:1). If one admits to the inspiration of the Biblical authors and that Matthew is not simply misquoting Hosea out of context, it is clear he means to identify Jesus with Israel. The nation of Israel was taken out of Egypt into the Promised Land, and this was recapitulated in the birth of Christ.

Another testimony to the conviction that Jesus is Israel comes from Paul. He writes: "Now the promises were made to Abraham and to his offspring. It does not say, 'And to offsprings,' referring to many, but

---

[37] Tremper Longman III, and Raymond B. Dillard, "Isaiah," *An Introduction to the Old Testament*, (Grand Rapids: Zondervan, 2006), 315.

[38] David P Scaer. *Discourses in Matthew: Jesus Teaches the Church.* (St. Louis: Concordia, 2004).

referring to one, 'And to your offspring,' who is Christ" (Gal. 3:16). The Abrahamic promise is the foundation for the blessings given to Israel throughout the Old Testament. Paul's point is that the true seed of Abraham is not the physical nation of Israel identified with the Mosaic administration, but ultimately is Christ himself. Those who inherit the promise of Abraham are adopted as members of spiritual Israel through incorporation into Christ who is the true Israel. This is why Paul argues: "And if you are Christ's, then you are Abraham's offspring, heirs according to promise" (Gal. 3:29). When placing the texts from Matthew's Gospel and Paul's epistles together, it becomes apparent that it was the belief of the early Apostles that Jesus himself is Israel.

The second point remains to be proven. It must be shown that the Abrahamic promises were in some sense, dependent upon the obedience of Israel. In Exodus 19, God tells Moses: "Now therefore, if you will indeed obey my voice and keep my covenant, you shall be my treasured possession among all peoples, for all the earth is mine; and you shall be to me a kingdom of priests and a holy nation" (Exod. 19:5). The promises of being a "holy nation," and a "kingdom of priest," are identified with obedience and covenant keeping of Israel. The New Testament identifies those who belong to Christ as both a holy nation and a kingdom of priests, demonstrating that the conditions had been fulfilled; Israel was obedient and kept the covenant.

After the conditions are laid out, the people of Israel agree to keep God's commandments. The people of Israel confess: "All that is spoken we will do" (Exod. 19:8). The conditionality of the Mosaic administration is expressed explicitly in Deuteronomy 11, which states:

> You shall therefore keep the whole commandment that I command you today, that you may be strong, and go in and take possession of the land that you are going over to possess, and that you may live long in the land that the LORD swore to your fathers to give to them and to their offspring, a land flowing with milk and honey... And if you will indeed obey my commandments that I command you today, to love the LORD your God, and to serve him with all your heart and with all your soul, he will give the rain for your land in its season, the early rain and the later rain, that you may gather in your grain and your wine and your oil. And he will give grass in your fields for your livestock, and you shall eat and be full. Take care lest your heart be deceived, and you turn aside and serve other gods and worship them; then the anger of the LORD will be kindled against you, and he will shut up the

> heavens, so that there will be no rain, and the land will yield no fruit, and you will perish quickly off the good land that the LORD is giving you. (Deut. 11:8-17)

The inheritance of the land promised to Abraham is in some sense dependent upon the people of Israel's fulfillment of the law. If they obeyed the covenant stipulations, they would be blessed; if they disobeyed, they would be punished. The remainder of Israel story in the Old Testament is consistent with this perspective, as the disobedience of the first generation of Israelites, including Moses, negated their entrance into the land. Similarly, the continued disobedience of Judah and Israel resulted in exile.

Jesus, as the true Israel, therefore necessarily had to obey God's law in order to gain the Abrahamic inheritance and receive the heavenly land due God's people. In Jesus, the entire story of Israel is recapitulated including his birth in Egypt, tempting in the wilderness, and exile at the cross. The difference, however, between Jesus and physical Israel is that Jesus obeyed where Israel disobeyed. While Israel failed to follow the covenant stipulations given through the law, Jesus obeyed them. And through his obedience to these stipulations, Christ overcame the curse of exile that was due to Israel's disobedience. When viewed in this manner, Christ's active obedience to the law (his role as faithful Israel), death (his taking the curse of exile due to disobedience upon himself), and resurrection (the fulfillment of the Abrahamic promise and end to the exile due to Christ's role as obedient Israel) form a compact and consistent unity with one another. Through faith, believers are incorporated into Christ and share in the blessings he won as the obedient seed of Abraham.

Conclusion

Now is a time when it is crucial to engage in the historic discussion about Christ's active obedience. We need not revert to Reformation-era arguments, which often missed important nuances in various texts. It has been shown in this essay that the classic defense of Christ's active obedience in view of Romans 5 is not exegetically tenable. However, rather than rejecting the doctrine, as do Forde and many other interpreters, this doctrine should be reclaimed on its Biblical grounds, because Jesus is the embodiment of Israel, and he was the perfectly faithful and righteous Son who, through his obedience, won the blessing of eternal life for his people. When this is recaptured, God's people can cling, not only to Christ's death as the grounds of their forgiveness, but also to his life as the grounds for the righteousness needed to avail before God the father. Let us then proclaim with the great hymn-writer Edward Mote that our hope is built on nothing less than Jesus' blood and righteousness.

Bibliography

Chrysostom, "The Epistle to the Romans," X.13., *Nicene and Post Nicene Fathers, First Series, Vol. 11*, Peabody: Hendrickson, 2004.

Cooper, Jordan. *The Righteousness of One: An Evaluation of Early Patristic Soteriology in Light of the New Perspective on Paul.* Eugene, OR: Wipf & Stock, 2013.

Forde, Gerhard. *Justification by Faith: A Matter of Life and Death* Mifflintown, PA: Sigler, 1991.

Forde, Gerhard. *Where God Meets Man.* Minneapolis: Augsburg, 1972.

Horton, Michael S. *Introducing Covenant Theology.* Grand Rapids: Baker, 2009.

Horton, Michael S. *Justified: Modern Reformation Essays on the Doctrine of Justification.* Escondido: Modern Reformation, 2010.

Husbands, Mark, and Daniel J. Treier. *Justification: What's at Stake in the Current Debates?* Downers Grove, IL: IVP, 2004.

Irenaeus, "Against Heresies," *Book V. XVII.3., Ante Nicene Fathers, Vol. 1.* Peabody: Hendrickson, 2004.

Johnson L., Gary and Guy P. Waters. *By Faith Alone: Answering the Challenges to the Doctrine of Justification.* Wheaton: Crossway, 2006.

Longman III, Tremper and Raymond B. Dillard, "Isaiah," *An Introduction to the Old Testament*, Grand Rapids: Zondervan, 2006.

Scaer, David P. *Discourses in Matthew: Jesus Teaches the Church.* St. Louis: Concordia, 2004.

Shepherd, Norman. "The Imputation of Christ's Active Obedience," in *Sandlin, Andrew P. A Faith That is Never Alone: A Response to Westminster Seminary California.* La Grange, CA: Kerygma, 2007.

Vickers, Brian. *Jesus' Blood and Righteousness: Paul's Theology of Imputation.* Wheaton: Crossway, 2006.

Gnadenwahlslehrstreit:
The American Lutheran Predestination
Controversy
By Lisa Cooper

Introduction

From the formation of the Formula of Concord and the other symbolical books, predestination was a contested doctrine among Lutherans because there was no clear positive teaching about it contained within those books.[1] With the rise of Calvinism, later Lutheran dogmaticians sought to better define and describe the doctrine, arriving at the phrase: *intuitu fidei*, or "in view of faith," which, in their minds, rightly defended against the Calvinistic error of unconditional election (absolute predestination), while affirming "the centrality of faith even in God's original election."[2] It also supposed to guard against synergism because "God elected persons in view of the faith that he himself granted to them. Though God's choice was conditional upon faith, this faith, like the predestinarian decree itself, belonged solely to God."[3]

In the early American Lutheran Church, the doctrine of predestination was bitterly debated, ultimately causing a schism to form between the Synodical Conference (the Missouri Synod and the Wisconsin Synod) and the rest of the American Lutheran bodies. This debate was referred to by those involved as *Gnadenwahlslehrstreit*, literally, election-of-grace doctrine controversy.[4] The main concern in the debate centered around the historic iteration of the doctrine of

---

[1] "Because Lutheran consensus was actually limited to the negative definition of the doctrine, and because of the danger of teaching a shallow election which is really no election under the guise of *intuitu fidei*, it was not strange that detailed discussion of this doctrine in the Missouri Synod should lead to trouble" Fred W. Meuser, The Formation of the American Lutheran Church (Eugene, Oregon: Wipf & Stock), 64.

[2] The Formation, 63.

[3] Peter J. Thuesen, Predestination: The American Career of a Contentious Doctrine (New York: Oxford University Press, 2009), 151. Also, it's important to make a note of why the version of intuitu fidei that arose in America was different from the Lutheran orthodox version. Thuesen asserts that, "Dogmatic formulas nevertheless were partially eclipsed in the eighteenth century as Lutherans, influenced by Pietism, emphasized the heart over the head in religion." Predestination, 152.

[4] Ibid., 150.

predestination: *intuitu fidei.* While the Ohio Synod and the Iowa Synod were concerned with preserving the phrase, contending that it was the historic and correct formulation of the doctrine of predestination, the Missouri Synod wanted to be rid of the phrase entirely in favor of Walther's new phrase: election unto faith.

Historical Overview

The doctrine of predestination was brought to the forefront of discussion among American Lutherans starting in the year 1868 when Pastor Huegli presented a paper at the meeting of the Wisconsin District that affirmed C. F. W. Walther's opinion that there is a definite election unto faith, as opposed to in view of faith.[5] Almost immediately, there were dissenters such as Iowa's Gottfried Fritschel who claimed that Walther's reformulation of the doctrine was a "gross insult to the Lutheran Church."[6] In May of 1872, Walther published a clarification about his articulation of the doctrine, arguing that he assented to the convictions of the old dogmaticians, believing their opinions on the predestination matter to be scriptural, but he "characterized as ambiguous the term '*intuitu fidei.*'"[7] After this perceived concession of Walther, five years passed before the doctrine was challenged again.

In 1877 at the meeting of the Western District, Walther brought up his new construction of the doctrine again, but this time he acquired a larger group of dissenters, among whom were Professor Asperheim and Professor F. A. Schmidt. By holding to *intuitu fidei,* Walther believed that the error of synergism was likely to infect the Lutheran church; for Walther, that formulation of the doctrine of predestination allows for man's nonresistance to be a cause of election. According to the minutes of the meeting:

> Walther does expressly call election a cause of faith (Thesis II) and denies the presence of any qualities in man which prompted God's foreknowledge to elect him (III); he also denies that the cause of the reprobation of the lost lies in God (IV). Walther warned that much of this doctrine is shrouded in mystery, and that not even all the revelations of God can be harmonized by man's mind. Therefore the mystery of election is simply to be accepted by the individual Christian who can

---

[5] A Brief History, 209; The Formation, 64.
[6] As quoted in Ibid., 64.
[7] J. L. Neve, A Brief History of the Lutheran Church in America (Brighton, Iowa: Just and Sinner, 2014), 209.

derive great assurance from the knowledge that God has elected him in Christ (V, VI).[8]

This was extremely controversial because he had denied that foreseen faith was the cause of election, thus departing from what had been taught previously in the Lutheran church. Because of this, and other statements of Walther that were perceived to be extreme, many pastors feared that Calvinism had infiltrated his articulation of the doctrine.[9]

Both President Strasen and Pastor H. A. Allwardt confronted Walther directly concerning the doctrine, and upon Pastor Schmidt's request, Walther consented to meet privately with him to discuss their differences further. Having come to no immediate conclusion, Schmidt and Walther agreed to postpone bringing the doctrine to public debate for one year until they could meet privately again. However, Walther decided to publicly discuss the issue at the meeting of the Western District in 1879, citing "certain people" of the Missouri Synod who disagreed with him. "[I]t soon became an open secret that he referred to Allwardt and Schmidt."[10] In response to the public attack, Schmidt began publishing "Altes und Neues," a monthly magazine "for the express purpose of opposing Walther's new construction."[11]

This controversy even affected Loy who, up until that point, had been a great supporter of Walther and the Missouri Synod. He, though despising the attitude with which Schmidt and Walther warred concerning the doctrine, published a long series of articles in the Lutheran Standard that denied Walther's charge that the formulation "*intuitu fidei*" detracted from salvation by grace. He even went so far as to join with the other dissenters by labeling Walther's interpretation "Calvinistic."[12]

The Missouri Synod pastors met in a general conference in Chicago from September 29 to October 5, 1880. At this meeting, "An overwhelming majority of the pastors declared themselves in full support of the views of Walther. When his opponents refused to

---

[8] The Formation, 65.

[9] Also, previously, Lutherans had not allowed for a discussion about the will of God concerning man's damnation, but only His will in electing them. This is where Walther's statements became extremely controversial, for example, he argued: "If then we would say to God, Why didst Thou not elect me? He would answer, Because I so willed. If now we were to ask further, Why then didst Thou so will? He would answer, It was simply the good pleasure of my will" Ibid., 65.

[10] A Brief History, 210.

[11] Ibid., 210.

[12] The Formation, 66.

withdraw their charge of Calvinism, the pro-Walther majority passed the following resolution: 'Resolved, that we regard all of the opponents who publicly attack us, no longer as brethren, but as enemies.'"[13] Because of this resolution, F. W. Stellhorn resigned from his position as professor at the Fort Wayne college and transferred to the Ohio Synod seminary in Columbus.[14]

The next year, the Missouri Synod adopted the thirteen theses of Walther concerning predestination. Those who opposed these theses called a separate meeting and left the Missouri Synod,[15] while the Minnesota and Wisconsin Synods sided with Missouri. The pastors who left the Missouri Synod soon joined with the Ohio Synod as the Northwestern District, and that same year the Ohio Synod split fellowship from Missouri. The formal separation of church fellowship came as a result of Missouri passing a resolution stating that anyone who disagreed with them regarding the doctrine of predestination were not to be recognized as a member of the Synodical Conference, and should not be consulted with concerning their involvement in the church.[16]

In the years 1903 through 1907, inter-synodical conferences brought up the predestination controversy again by debating two main questions: 1) "What is the Lutheran doctrine of predestination?"; and 2) "What do the Scriptures teach concerning predestination?"[17] The Norwegian Lutheran Synod and the United Norwegian Lutheran Church sought to unify, and in doing so, they had together settled on The Madison Theses (also known as The Norwegian Articles of Agreement) in which they outlined what was necessary for church fellowship concerning the doctrine of predestination.[18] In the settled theses, they affirmed two forms to predestination, stating: "[I]t is well known that two forms of the doctrine have been used, both of which

---

[13] Ibid., 66-67.

[14] Ibid., 67.

[15] According to A Brief History, there were five who voted against these theses, but The Formation explains that six pastors refused to assent to the theses at this meeting. The Formation also explains that the reason for their dissension was because "they felt that the theses did not accurately express what Missouri had been espousing since 1877." A Brief History, 210-211; The Formation, 67.

[16] A Brief History, 211; The Formation, 67-68.

[17] Ibid., 212.

[18] Leander S. Keyser, Election and Conversion: A Frank Discussion of Dr. Pieper's Book on "Conversion and Election," with Suggestions for Lutheran Concord and Union on Another Basis (Burlington, Iowa: The German Literary Board), https://archive.org/details/electionconvers00keys, 6.

have been recognized as correct in the orthodox Lutheran Church," and "neither of these two forms of the doctrine contradicts any doctrine revealed in the Word of God." [19] Dr. F. Pieper sought to warn them against accepting the theses as written,[20] by writing a brochure, called Conversion and Election and sending it to every Lutheran minister in America.[21] An extensive treatment of the arguments regarding the doctrine of predestination from the beginning of the debate would be too extensive for a paper of this length, so the remainder of this paper deals with Pieper's specific argumentation for the Missourian doctrine in 1913, and the response, Election and Conversion, written by Leander Keyser in 1914. With these two works, the heated debate dissipated, and pastors, instead of arguing over synodical lines, aligned themselves with whatever synod best represented their views about predestination and church fellowship.

The Madison Theses/The Norwegian Articles of Agreement

To aptly convey the context into which Pieper was writing, it is important to first know what was written in The Madison Theses. These theses were adopted at Madison, Wisconsin in 1912 after much debate.[22] First, the settlement affirmed both the doctrine of predestination outlined in the Eleventh Article of the Formula of Concord (the "first form"), and Pontoppidan's Explanation (the "second form").[23] The theses go on to define the first form by saying that some Lutherans "make the doctrine of Election to comprise the entire salvation of the elect from the calling to the glorification...and teach an election 'to salvation through the sanctification by the Spirit and faith in the truth'"[24] The second form teaches that, "God has ordained to eternal life all those who from eternity He foresaw would accept the proffered grace, believe in Christ, and remain steadfast in this faith unto the end."[25] Both of these formulations of the doctrine were to be regarded as orthodox, and a differing opinion would not be regarded as grounds for division in church fellowship.

---

[19]F. Pieper, Conversion and Election: A Plea for a United Lutheranism in America (Saint Louis, Missouri: Concordia Publishing House, 1913), 7, 8.

[20] A Brief History, 212.

[21] Ibid., 212.

[22] "Madison Settlement" Christian Cyclopedia (Saint Louis, Missouri: Concordia Publishing House, 2000). http://cyclopedia.lcms.org/display.asp?t1=M&word=MADISONSETTLEMENT, 1.

[23] Conversion and Election, 7.

[24] Ibid., 7.

[25] Ibid., 8.

The Theses continue, citing common arguments waged against both forms of the doctrine, and rejecting both synergism and Calvinism. First, they overtly condemn synergism by rejecting: 1) the idea that there is something in man that merits his election; 2) that God has taken into account man's good conduct in electing him; 3) that faith in Christ is dependent upon man's choosing; and 4) that as a result of grace offered to an unregenerate man, he can then decide for grace and subsequently be saved.[26]

Next, the Theses reject Calvinism. They do this by condemning the doctrines that state: 1) that God acts "arbitrarily and without motive" in election, choosing some and passing by others; 2) that God has two wills in election, one that calls all people, and still another that issues a more effective call to the elect; 3) that God is actively responsible for those who are ultimately condemned; and 4) that a believer can be absolutely sure of his election and salvation, where instead, he should be absolutely sure of his faith.[27] Bearing the claims of the Madison Theses in mind, the conversation between Pieper and Keyser makes much more sense.

Church Fellowship/Occasion for Writing
The question of what determines church fellowship was fundamental to the discussion concerning predestination. While Pieper, along with the whole Missouri Synod, maintained that the only way to engage in fraternal church relations was to have complete doctrinal agreement, Keyser took a much more loose approach, claiming that there are some doctrines (like the doctrine of Election) which cannot be dogmatized

---

[26] Ibid., 8-9. These reflect and paraphrase many of the Antitheses or Negative Theses written in the Formula of Concord, Article XI on Election. The introduction to that section of Article XI reads as follows: "[W]e believe and maintain that those who present the teaching of God's gracious election to eternal life either in such a way that troubled Christians cannot find comfort in it but are driven to faintheartedness or despair, or in such a way that the impenitent are strengthened in their arrogance, are not preaching this teaching according to the Word and will of God but rather according to their own reason and at the instigation of the accursed devil, because (as the Apostle testifies) 'whatever was written was written for our instruction, so that by steadfastness and by the comfort of the Scriptures we might have hope' [Rom. 25:4]." (FC SD XI.16)

[27] Ibid., 9. These reflect and paraphrase many of the Antitheses or Negative Theses written in the Formula of Concord, Article XI on Election.

and used as a basis of division in the Lutheran church.[28] For Keyser and the rest of the General Synod, agreement on the biblical doctrines that directly concern salvation by grace through faith was enough for church fellowship. This would simply not do for Pieper, or anyone else in the Missouri Synod.

Pieper's goal in writing was to convert those Norwegian bodies to the "correct" and therefore only Scriptural understanding of election.[29] It was not enough that the Norwegian bodies agreed that both forms of the doctrine were satisfactory for Lutheran orthodoxy (with the provision that the second form was "not to be used in an effort to explain the mystery involved in the doctrine of election").[30] Pieper writes: "For the union of the Lutheran Church in America with reference to the doctrine of Conversion and Election nothing more is needed than to bring the teaching which men profess in public into harmony with that which, as Christians, they believe in their heart."[31] Had the Missouri Synod consented to a looser version of church fellowship, Pieper would not have written this book, nor would there have been a division among the synods because of this debate.

Keyser, however, sought to undo what Pieper had done in calling the Norwegian bodies to amend their Madison theses. He wanted to not only deal with the doctrine in Pieper's book, but he also wanted to make it clear that the doctrine of predestination "ought not be made the ground of division among Lutherans who truly accept the Word of God and the Lutheran Confessions, even though they cannot understand all things in the same way."[32] Keyser wanted a united, fraternal Lutheranism based on a positive confession of faith, while Pieper wanted a united, doctrinally pure Lutheranism; both men had a desire for a united Lutheranism in America, but the grounds for unification were entirely different.

The Main Disagreements
The main disagreements about predestination are not limited to the term "in view of faith." It is not only a dispute over a faulty phrase, but

---

[28] "No body of men should presume to dogmatize [the mysteries of the eternal decrees of the Godhead] in such a way as to exclude from church-fellowship any of their Lutheran brethren." Ibid., 7.

[29] "[W]e believe that the Norwegian church bodies will concur with us in declaring that the second conception, which is not found in Scripture, and, for this reason, is not professed in the Lutheran Confessions, ought to be stricken from their articles of church union." Ibid., 13.

[30] Ibid., 20.

[31] Ibid., 51.

[32] Election and Conversion, 7.

is grounded in a fundamental difference in understanding how to reconcile Scripture passages about predestination with themselves. This brings up the question: wherein lies the mystery? Because the Formula of Concord speaks ill of taking Scripture passages concerning predestination past their plain meaning, it allows for a theology that is not completely reconciled.[33] This is why historic Lutheranism affirms both *universalis gratia* and *sola gratia*. This defends against the errors of synergism and Calvinism. Pieper seeks to maintain the mystery concerning God's eternal decrees, while Keyser believes the mystery to be found not in the eternal decrees, but in the call of God to unregenerate people. In conjunction with this, the *ordo salutis* (order of salvation) proves to be a dividing factor among these two men. Pieper speaks of God's call, illumination, regeneration, and so on, as a logical order, while Keyser makes the order of salvation temporal. This drastically influences how both men discuss the doctrine of predestination. This list is not exhaustive, but it does provide a thorough basis for understanding the predestination controversy.

"In View of Faith"

The primary concern of Missouri was the use of the phrase "*intuitu fidei.*" As was noted in the previous historical treatment, this is where the whole debate began. According to Missouri, the phrase was fundamentally flawed and was not in concert with Scripture, the Formula of Concord, or the historical teachings of the Lutheran church. Although *intuitu fidei* had become the common way of discussing the doctrine of predestination, the Missouri Synod desired to strike the phrase from common use because it could lead to a synergistic view of predestination. Pieper does admit that there are reasonable ways of explaining the second form of the doctrine that are in agreement with the first form, however, he argues, "[I]n that case everybody will grant that we must apply the rule: *Tene mentem, corrige linguam*, that is, Keep your correct thought, but drop your faulty expression."[34] He goes on to

---

[33] "The latent tension in the Formula between predestination and the universal grace of the gospel left a door ajar for future debates. Moreover, Melanchthon's nagging question remained: was human faith of absolutely no consequence in God's choice of the elect? In struggling with this issue, Lutherans faced a particular dilemma. If faith were of no consequence, then God seemed to loom as a fearfully arbitrary monarch. But if faith—conceived of as a human "work"—did matter, then the cardinal Lutheran principle of sola gratia (grace alone) was compromised." Predestination, 151.

[34] Conversion and Election, 14; "In the historical excursus (chap. IX) we have furnished the evidence to show that the dogmaticians of the seventeenth century, who use the formula 'election in view of faith,' while

affirm that the so-called "new" way of speaking of the doctrine in Missouri (unto faith) was not, in fact, new. He claims that:

> The position which is in accordance with Scripture, and, hence, is the only correct one from the theological view-point, viz., the position which maintains both sola gratia and *universalis gratia*, without diminishing the force of either, has been expressed, as far as we can see, only three times in public documents issued by churches, and recorded in the history of the Christian Church: in the decrees of the Synod of Orange in 529, in the 11th Article of the Form of Concord, in 1570, and in the 13 Theses of the Missouri Synod, in 1881.[35]

This is a bold claim to make. In the history of the Lutheran church, predestination had only been spoken of correctly three times. This, for Pieper, was not a revolution in doctrine (because Missouri was opposed to revolutions in doctrine), but it was a revival of proper doctrine that had been obscured by the faulty language of *intuitu fidei.*

Keyser, however, sees no issue with the phrase. In fact, he vehemently promotes it over against the Missouri doctrine of election unto faith. By taking away the language of *intuitu fidei*, Keyser believes that Pieper downplays the importance of faith in the life of the Christian. He writes: "[Pieper] seems to treat faith as if it were so insignificant a thing that it would be absurd to think that it could in the least have affected God's eternal self-determinations."[36] Keyser claims that he upholds justification as the central doctrine by believing that we are elected in view of faith, while Pieper compromises the centrality of justification in favor of election unto faith.[37]   In the Missourian

---

combatting at the same time the synergism of Latermann and Musaeus, do not present the same doctrine as the American champions of this formula. We have, however, added distinctly that assent to this historical excursus is not required for unity in doctrine. As regards this particular phrase, *intuitu fidei*, we have shown that, even when there is no synergistic meaning underlying this term, it must in no wise be given the right of existence within the Christian Church, because, if this is done, the Scripture-principle is certainly violated." Ibid., 147.

[35] Ibid., 5.

[36] Election and Conversion, 25.

[37] According to Keyser, Conversion and Election "puts into a minor place the material, chief and regulative principle of the Reformation, namely, justification by faith." Instead, "[T]he doctrine of divine decrees, the divine sovereignty, election, predestination" becomes the principal doctrine. Keyser goes on: "Even faith is treated meagerly, is subjected to election, is taken quite

formulation "man is not elected in view of the fact that he accepts Christ by faith, but he both has faith and is justified because he has been elected unto salvation from eternity by a mysterious decree."[38] Despite Keyser being vocal about how Missouri was not promoting Calvinism—though that charge was waged against them by many—he was concerned that by removing the phrase *intuitu fidei* from the discussion of predestination that it would inevitably lead to the Calvinistic doctrine of irresistible grace. He writes: "According to Missouri, each individual who is finally saved was predestined unto faith, which must mean that when he was elected, his faith was elected with him. That view eliminates every vestige of freedom from faith, and therefore spells 'irresistible grace.'"[39] Freedom to choose is foundational to Keyser's theology.

Wherein Lies the Mystery?
Along with the debate concerning the wording of the doctrine of predestination, one of the other fundamental differences between Pieper and Keyser's treatments of the doctrine is grounded in what mystery is Scripturally warranted. On many occasions in the Formula of Concord, Article XI, there are warnings against attempting to peer into God's inscrutable will and foreknowledge, attempting to reconcile where Scripture is silent.[40] Both Pieper and Keyser believe that their doctrinal articulation maintains that mystery while still upholding the truth of the infallibility of the Scriptures.

Pieper retains the mystery of God's will in promoting both *universalis gratia*, and sola gratia. He explains the fundamental problem of universalis gratia when he writes: "The Scriptures teach, on the one

---

out of the sphere of freedom, and is so misconceived as to be made a mechanical thing, instead of the ethical and spiritual act it is always represented to be in the Bible and the Lutheran Confessions." Ibid., 22-23.

[38] Ibid., 23.

[39] Ibid., 37.

[40] The following quote purports from our Confessions expresses this mystery, and calls us to look to Christ, not to the mysteries of the eternal councils of God: "[I]f a person wishes to think or speak about the election and *praedestinatio* (or preordination) of God's children to eternal life correctly and profitably, one should as a matter of course refrain from speculation over the naked, secret, hidden, inscrutable foreknowledge of God. On the contrary, one should focus on how God's counsel, intention, and preordination in Jesus Christ...is revealed to us through the Word. This means that the entire teaching of God's intention, counsel, will, and preordination concerning our redemption, calling, justification, and salvation must be taken as a unity" (FC SD XI.13-14).

hand, that the grace of God in Christ is extended to all men alike, and, on the other hand, that there is no difference among men, since all are in the same state of total depravity and in the same guilt before God, and their conduct over against the saving grace of God is equally evil."[41] This does not make sense from a human standpoint. How is it that God can equally offer grace to all sinful people without either converting all people, or allowing all people to reject him? Is the grace God sends to all people divided so that some receive more grace than others? In response to this, he explains: "The Scriptures teach that some are saved merely by the grace of God, and the rest are lost solely by their own guilt."[42] In believing that some are saved by grace alone, but at the same time some are lost by their own rejection of that grace, Pieper allows what appears to be a contradiction.

This, however, is not a contradiction; both truths are affirmed in Scripture, even though they are not perfectly reconcilable in our own logic. The Formula of Concord speaks of this very tension:

> As God preordained in his counsel that the Holy Spirit would call, enlighten, and convert the elect through the Word and that he would justify and save all those who accept Christ through true faith, so also he concluded in his counsel that he would harden, reject, and condemn all those whom he called through the Word when they spurn the Word and resist and persist in resisting the Holy Spirit, who wants to exercise his power in them and be efficacious through the Word. This is why 'many are called and few are chosen' [Matt. 22:14] (FC SD XI.40).

It is clear, then, that the language "election unto faith," seeks to uphold this tension without claiming to reconcile it.

To deal with the question Pieper raises about why some people are finally saved and others finally lost, Keyser cites scriptures such as John 3:16-19, "God so loved the world that he gave His only begotten Son that whosoever believeth on Him should not perish, but have everlasting life...He that believeth on Him is not judged; he that believeth not hath been judged already because he hath not believed on the only begotten Son of God." He explains, "Here Christ makes it very clear why some are saved and others lost; the former believe on Christ; the latter do not believe on Him."[43] This is where the language of *intuitu fidei* comes into play. Because God foresees and foreknows the

---

[41] Ibid., 21.

[42] Ibid., 21.

[43] Election and Conversion, 32, emphasis retained from primary text.

faith of the elect, God's eternal decrees are not a mystery in the same way that Pieper sees them to be. Keyser asserts, "Christ does not posit the difference in the destiny of saints and sinners in God's eternal decree, but in man's acceptance or rejection of the gospel."[44]

This is why, for Keyser, the mystery in the doctrine of predestination stems from the fact that God calls and demands faith of unregenerate people when there can be no faith because they are "dead in sin" according to Scripture. But, at the same time, those who are saved are saved by grace alone. It is not in God's decrees, but rather in how mankind accepts or rejects the grace offered to them in the call of the Gospel that raises a red flag for Keyser. He writes:

> On the one hand, the Bible plainly teaches that the unconverted man is dead in sin, totally unable to believe on Christ; on the other hand, it commands, urges and entreats him, while still unconverted, to believe on Christ, and threatens him with dire punishment if he refuses. Shall we stop here, throw up our hands, and call it an inscrutable mystery, as the Synodical Conference brethren do relative to election, and thus represent the Bible as a bundle of contradictions...or shall we think more acutely and exaltedly, and see whether we will not find the Bible throughout to be a book of wondrous beauty, of perfect harmony, of organic unity?[45]

Here Keyser identifies what seems to be a contradiction, but in the next breath claims that it must be reconciled logically in order to uphold the doctrine of Scriptural inerrancy. He has already solved the mystery of why some are saved and others lost with *intuitu fidei*, now he must solve this tension: how is it that God can demand faith of people who cannot say yes? He answers in the form of another question: "Will not God accomplish His purpose? Is He going to call on dead men to wake up and accept salvation, and yet leave them utterly dead?"[46] Keyser then posits a temporal *ordo salutis* to answer this question. By separating out Illumination (which corresponds to the mind), Conversion (which corresponds to the will), and Regeneration (which

---

[44] Ibid., 33.
[45] Ibid., 45.
[46] Ibid., 48.

corresponds to the spirit), Keyser seeks to reconcile sola gratia and the responsibility of the human will.[47]

The Ordo Salutis

Another difference between Pieper and Keyser is how they interpret the *ordo salutis*. This is foundational to their whole theology—not just the doctrine of predestination. While Pieper sees conversion as an instantaneous reality wherein all benefits of salvation are received, Keyser sees each aspect of conversion, and those leading up to conversion (the call, illumination, conversion, regeneration, justification, etc.) as taking place temporally to allow for a specific time wherein the unregenerate has enough grace to make a decision to reject or accept the grace offered to him. This is how Keyser solves the above-mentioned mystery of human responsibility and sola gratia.

Although Pieper believes that the Holy Spirit does impress upon unbelievers prior to conversion from without, he directly condemns the teaching that the unregenerate can—even by God's grace—do anything to help achieve salvation from within. These acts of preparation by the Holy Spirit are the only way in which it is appropriate to talk about conversion being a process. Pieper quotes Walther, saying: "Conversion, indeed, does not occur ordinarily without several preparatory phenomena (*Vorgaenge*) within man, and in this sense conversion is accomplished by degrees, gradually; but conversion itself in every case occurs in an instant."[48] However, to guard against the false teaching that can occur if these preparatory acts are not discussed carefully, Pieper quotes Calovius:

> 1. To assume holy thoughts previous to regeneration, conversion, and faith, is pure and genuine Pelagianism. 2. To assume holy motions previous to the work of the Holy Spirit, places the effect before the cause. 3. To assume in the corrupt heart of non-converted man a pious longing, amounts to producing good fruit while the tree is still corrupt. 4. To imagine, in him, a struggle of the flesh with the Spirit, is a contradiction in terms. 5. To assume the beginnings of faith where regeneration has not occurred, when, in fact, faith

---

[47] For the sake of organization, I have separated out how Keyser answers this question in the *ordo salutis* section, even though it technically could fit under either heading.

[48] Conversion and Election, 109.

originates through regeneration, is the same as assuming the child to exist before the father.[49]

It is therefore of utmost importance that the distinction between the Holy Spirit working from within and from without are not conflated because "A will 'prepared' in such a way that it can decide in favor of grace, and can will grace, is already converted."[50] This stands in stark contrast to Keyser's view of conversion.

Another question arises in the discussion of preparatory acts—the question of the possibility of conversion. Pieper affirms this phraseology because: "The Scriptures teach *gratia sufficiens*, that is to say, it teaches that God operates through the call in such a manner and to such an extent that all hearers of the Word 'may be enlightened, converted, and saved,' and that no hearer remains unconverted by reason of some deficiency in the operations of divine grace or by reason of a lack of gracious intent on the part of God."[51] It is not, as synergists would maintain, that the possibility of grace is a limitation. That is to say, that God makes conversion possible, but instead of God supplying sufficient grace to make it happen, a person must actualize this grace by accepting it, making it truly saving grace. Because conversion is an instantaneous reality for Pieper, all of the benefits of salvation are bestowed on the believer at the time of conversion. Therefore there is no state of an unbeliever where they have enough grace to make a decision either for or against the grace that has been offered to them.[52] The unbeliever who would then truly pray to God is therefore no longer an unbeliever, but has a regenerated heart that leans on Christ for salvation.

As Pieper warns, Keyser's doctrine of *intuitu fidei* lead him to a doctrine of human responsibility wherein he claims that all people, because God's call is universal, must have some opportunity where they can choose to accept grace or reject it. Even though he vehemently condemns the allegations of being a synergist, Keyser believes it to be fundamental to the Christian faith that the human make a decision for Christ. To deal with the accusations that his position negates sola gratia, he asserts: "Even if God did, by virtue of his foreknowledge, elect believers unto salvation, in view of their faith, it would not destroy the heavenly doctrine of sola gratia, because faith simply accepts the gratuity from the hands of the God of love and mercy." He goes on:

---

[49] Ibid., 113.
[50] Ibid., 108.
[51] Ibid., 120, emphasis retained from primary text.
[52] Ibid., 109.

"Surely, if God honors faith so much as to make it the vehicle of justification in time, it would not derogate from His honor for Him to have taken it into consideration in the counsels of eternity. God must have thought a good deal of faith, or He would not have elected from eternity that men should be justified and saved through faith."[53] This is the basis for Keyser's view of the *ordo salutis*. He begins by making faith the "vehicle of justification in time," that is then "taken into account" by God in eternity.[54] Pieper claims that this kind of thinking makes election the antecedent of faith, thus making it a work of man that then changes God's eternal decree.[55] How does this work out practically if, according to Keyser, we are not elected based on our good conduct, but only by the grace of God? He explains that, "A 'gift' must be accepted, and accepted freely, or it is not a gift. Something that is forced upon you is not a gift. We must, therefore, differ from Missouri's position, because its teachings slight and minify God's gracious work in the preparatory movements leading to conversion."[56]

These preparatory movements, for Keyser, are not to be discussed devoid of grace and the work of the Holy Spirit. Keyser separates out the *ordo salutis* first with the call. The call of God is extended to all people, then, "Simultaneously with the Call, or straightaway following it, no matter which, there goes another most gracious work of God—Illumination." "The Illumination comes by God's grace in two ways: First, by the law; second, by the gospel."[57] In this illumination, the unregenerate man is able to see that he is in desperate need of grace. Keyser explains that illumination is an act of the Holy Spirit "whereby He produces awakening, enlightenment, knowledge of sin and the way of salvation, and also effects a certain enablement of the will, thus making the sinner a responsible agent respecting his

---

[53] Election and Conversion, 28.

[54] "God has elected sinners in view of the use they will make of divinely imparted and enabled freedom at every point in the Order of Salvation, from the first moment of the Call to the final transfer to glory in heaven. In this process faith plays a large and determining part; yet it does not enter into the prevenient acts, but is implanted in regeneration. Thus *intuitu fidei* is an expression that can be retained for convenience, if it is remembered how it is produced, and what acts of the Holy Spirit precede it." Ibid., 114.

[55] "But this correct doctrine does not find expression in the second conception of Election. The formula, 'Election in view of steadfast faith,' rather conveys the thought that faith, faith persevering unto the end of life, is an antecedent of election" Conversion and Election, 15.

[56] Election and Conversion, 51-52.

[57] Ibid., 49.

personal salvation."[58] At this point, the unregenerate has enough prevenient grace that he can pray to God and ask for help in saving him. Keyser writes: "Now, if the sinner will pray to God for help, God will, through added prevenient grace, enable him freely to cease his resistance, freely to surrender himself to God alone; yes, even to cease trying to save himself, and simply let God and God alone, save him."[59] Furthermore, Keyser asserts that there must at this point be a decision on the part of the believer:

> [T]here must come a time in the process when God's Spirit enables the sinner to choose to let himself be saved or not, as the Scripture teaches: 'Choose ye this day whom ye will serve' (Josh 24:15); 'How long halt ye between two opinions? If God be God, follow Him; if Baal, then follow him' (1 Kings 18:21, spoken to unregenerate men). If such a moment of option does not come to the sinner before conversion, then conversion is forced upon him.[60]

The antinomy, then, that Keyser allows to stand is that somehow God allows man to make a decision for or against grace, but it is still by the grace of God that he is saved.

Conclusion

Ultimately, the Norwegian bodies merged in 1917, despite Pieper's call to amend the Madison Agreement, thus forming the Norwegian Lutheran Church of America that supported both formulations of the doctrine.[61] However, there was a small contingent of Norwegian Lutherans who opposed *intuitu fidei*, and refused the merger. These Lutherans formed the Evangelical Lutheran Synod in 1918.[62] This controversy helped solidify the Missouri Synod's staunch beliefs about

---

[58] Ibid., 60.

[59] Ibid., 63. "[W]e reject the view that the unconverted man can 'co-operate toward his conversion;' the word 'co-operate' is, to our mind, too strong a word at that stage; the called and illumined sinner can do nothing toward his conversion; he can simply let God save him; that much ability God gives in the call and illumination—to be passive in God's hands; even as long as he tries to save himself, he will balk God's efforts to save him." (95)

[60] Ibid., 100-101.

[61] Predestination, 166. The Norwegian Lutheran Church of America was eventually absorbed in the Evangelical Lutheran Church in America (ELCA) merger.

[62] The ELS—although small—still exists today, and is known for their vehement support of the formulation that we are elected unto faith. Ibid., 167.

church fellowship, and set them up in many ways to be somewhat isolated in the landscape of Lutheran synods in America.[63]

As with any controversy, there are many different opinions, many of which fall somewhere between the two presented here. There were many theologians at the time of this debate who would have vehemently disagreed with Keyser's articulation of the doctrine of *intuitu fidei*, but would have still opposed the new language of Walther and Pieper. That being said, after the Madison Theses were accepted and the Norwegian groups formed, the doctrine of predestination ceased being publicly debated.

The doctrines of conversion and election have fallen out of focus for many Lutherans in America today. The specificity and nuance with which these men argued their position has been lost. The controversy is hardly talked about, showing up in strikingly few history books. On a lay level, it is more than often glossed over as a topic, or articulated as being somewhere in the middle between Calvinism and synergism. "Single predestination" is often used as a colloquial short-hand to explain predestination from a confessional Lutheran standpoint. It is, however, imperative to uphold the Scriptural truths of *sola gratia* and *gratia universalis* without compromise. These truths, in my opinion, are best supported with the language of "election unto faith." There is great comfort in a proper understanding of the doctrines of conversion and election, despite the mystery.

---

[63] "[T]he predestination controversy brought about a 'radical change' in the attitude of the Missourians toward other Lutherans. Walther's dogged insistence on *reine Lehre*—pure doctrine, defined on his terms—fostered a spirit of isolationism that continued after his death." Ibid., 164.

Bibliography

Keyser, Leander, S. *Election and Conversion: A Frank Discussion of Dr. Pieper's Book on "Conversion and Election," with Suggestions for Lutheran Concord and Union on Another Basis* (Burlington, Iowa: The German Literary Board), https://archive.org/details/electionconvers00keys.

"Madison Settlement" *Christian Cyclopedia* (Saint Louis, Missouri: Concordia Publishing House, 2000). http://cyclopedia.lcms.org/display.asp?t1=M&word=MADISON SETTLEMENT

Meuser, Fred W. *The Formation of the American Lutheran Church* (Eugene, Oregon: Wipf & Stock).

Neve, J. L. *A Brief History of the Lutheran Church in America* (Brighton, Iowa: Just and Sinner, 2014).

Pieper, F. *Conversion and Election: A Plea for a United Lutheranism in America* (Saint Louis, Missouri: Concordia Publishing House, 1913).

The Book of Concord: The Confessions of the Evangelical Lutheran Church, ed. Robert Kolb and Timothy J. Wengert, trans. Charles Aranad, Eric Gritcsch, Robert Kolb, William Russell, James Schaff, Jane Strohl, Timothy J. Wengert (Minneapolis, Minnesota: Fortress Press, 2000).

The Lutheran Study Bible: English Standard Version (Saint Louis: Concordia Publishing House, 2001).

Thuesen, Peter J. *Predestination: The American Career of a Contentious Doctrine* (New York: Oxford University Press, 2009).

Book Reviews

Trueman, Carl R. *Luther on the Christian Life: Cross and Freedom.* (Wheaton: Crossway, 2015).
Review by Jordan Cooper

At first glance, it seems to be a rather odd choice for a Presbyterian minister to write a book on Martin Luther. Like Bonhoeffer and C.S. Lewis, every tradition seems to claim Luther as their own, and thus books on Luther often emphasize the particular aspects of his theology that are consistent with the author's views. Because of his Calvinism, one might expect that there might be an inordinate amount of space devoted to Luther's *Bondage of the Will*, and little discussion of Luther's sacramentology. Thankfully, none of these fears are realized within this book. Trueman offers an accurate and honest picture of Luther, acknowledging his own disagreements with the Reformer.

This book is written from a popular perspective, rather than a particularly academic one, and is immensely readable. One will not get bogged down in footnotes, though it is apparent throughout the work that Trueman is very well informed of Luther's thought as well as contemporary Luther scholarship. Trueman begins the book with a brief overview of Luther's life, contending that his life must be understood in order for one to comprehend the nature of his thought. He then proceeds to extrapolate various aspects of Luther's theology throughout the following chapters.

Like most works on Luther, Trueman spends a majority of his writing on Luther's early writings. He devotes a large amount of space to Luther's Heidelberg Disputation, and his 1520 reformation treatises. Yet, Trueman does recognize the importance of the late Luther, and contends that one has an imbalanced view of the Reformer by neglecting the post 1525 writings. He argues that this difference in approach is due to Luther's early eschatological expectations which were not realized. Trueman, rightly I think, argues that the later Luther emphasizes good works due to his controversies with the antinomians, and even teaches something like a "third use of the law," even if that specific terminology is not utilized. These topics are discussed in his chapter "Luther on Christian Righteousness," which is the most original contribution Trueman makes in this work. He demonstrates that Luther does not view sanctification merely as "getting used to justification," but as a process of spiritual growth. Because of Luther's heavy emphasis on the distinction between law and gospel, this aspect of Luther's theology is often ignored.

As a historian, Trueman expounds Luther in light of his late medieval context. This allows Trueman to deal more honestly with categories like "theologies of glory," and "theology of the cross." He explains them as an expansion and rejection of various aspects of medieval theology and piety, while not arguing that they are overarching theological categories by which all theology must be judged (a problem many contemporary Lutheran theologians have). He also places the *Bondage of the Will* in its proper context without trying to prove that Luther was a double-predestinarian Calvinist. In his chapter on the sacraments, Trueman clearly articulates a Lutheran approach to baptism and the Lord's Supper, while acknowledging his disagreement with Luther on these particular points. He gives some helpful clarifications to try to help Protestants gain a sympathetic understanding to Luther's concern on these points.

There are two primary issues with this work. First, Trueman makes the contention that Luther's sermons follow a strict law-gospel structure. He writes: "The modern reader of Luther's sermons will probably also notice that, after a while, the sermons all start to seem much the same. That is because the law-gospel pattern is reflected in them all" (95). While Luther certainly preaches both law and gospel in nearly all of his sermons, he does not adhere to a strict sermon structure. At times, Luther ends his sermons with commands. For example, in a 1535 sermon on covetousness, Luther ends his message saying:

> In this example of the rich man and poor Lazarus, we have a terrifying and earnest lesson against covetousness. It is a particularly shameful evil at work among greedy, loveless people, full of great injustice, thwarting all the fruits of the gospel. The Lord rebukes this evil, therefore, for good reason, especially since it adorns itself as a virtue, refusing to be viewed as sin. If we find ourselves in it, may God help us, so that we come free of it. Amen.[1]

This is not merely the late Luther, but it is the early Luther who preached his sermon on the *Two Kinds of Righteousness*, which utilizes a justification then sanctification structure. In contrast to Trueman's claim, Luther cannot clearly be placed in one particular mode of preaching, though the law-gospel structure is certainly prominent.

---

[1] Luther, Martin. *Complete Sermons of Martin Luther.* (Grand Rapids: Baker, 2000), 6:240.

The second problem in this volume is Trueman's contention that Luther is in accord with late medieval Nominalism and rejects essentialist ontology for one centered on God's Word as a performative speech-act. This is a common contention in Luther scholarship, but I have not found such claims compelling. Luther's most oft-cited sources (Tauler, the *Theologica Germanica*, etc.) are rather Platonic in outlook. Luther also approved several of Melanchthon's works which utilized traditional Greek philosophical categories.

Though not a perfect work on Luther, this book is a helpful introduction to the Reformer's thought. Trueman's approach is balanced, and he emphasizes the most important areas of Luther's life and thought in an immensely readable and practical volume.

Sunukjian, Donald R. *Invitation to Philippians: Building a Great Church Through Humility* (Biblical Preaching for the Contemporary Church). Weaver Book Company, 2014.
By Rich Shields

When deciding which books to read, I try to find ones that will enhance what I know, broaden my perspective, or teach me something new. Unfortunately, this book did none of those things. The series title, "Biblical Preaching for the Contemporary Church," suggested that there would be helps for those preaching to dig into the book, in this case, Philippians. Instead it was a series of sermons based on Philippians.

At first reading the sermons might appear generally Biblical. He offers the key thoughts of the letter in each sermon. Taken overall, he covers what Paul highlights (but there is a subtle and seductive shift). The reader has to keep in mind that this is a survey of the letter, not an in-depth study. As such it might work as an introduction for the congregation to engage in further discovery of the riches of Philippians. It didn't seem to encourage the congregation to take a further look into Paul's letter.

One challenge of reading a sermon vs. hearing a sermon is the difference in style. I appreciate the comments in the Preface, "But I have tried my best to retain their oral flavor—I've wanted them to still sound close to the way we talk. This means there will be incomplete sentences, colloquial and idiomatic language, and other features of the spoken word." P. 7) In this case the author succeeded and he is to be commended.

There are some legalistic, yet inconsistent problems in the book. Here are some brief selections:

> That's one way you can be confident that people are committed to the work of the Lord—their homes are available. (p. 7)

> You can be confident that God is at work in someone when you see that person stand up for the truth and willing to take the heat for it. (p. 8)

> You can have confidence that God is in people's lives when they give their money. (p. 9)

There are too many counter examples in real life to use these as the criteria "that God is at work." But even worse, sanctification becomes the criteria of the Christian life, even above justification. Perhaps the following quote best demonstrates the trend toward moralism: "The answer is: The more love we have, the better choices we will make and the better people we will become." (p. 16)

This confuses Law and Gospel and highlights sanctification over justification. And then he contradicts himself in Chapter 10, "The Christian Subculture: Righteous of Rubbish." He wrote:

> What is this tragedy that occurs if we let someone impose their rules and regulations on us, pressuring us into their spiritual lifestyle? What is the harm, the damage we suffer when we begin to think that following someone else's codes will make us more righteous in God's eyes? (p. 77)

The corrective he offers is really the same with a different coating:

> What defines you as belonging to God is not some external behavior. What defines you is the internal presence of the Spirit of God. He's totally changed everything about you and has become part of your life.... You're pleasing to him not because you belong to a particular party, but because you act justly and fairly and mercifully toward all those around you. (p. 79)

The author leaves the listener/reader in a predicament. It's not what we do, but what we do that matters? I think this misses the entire thrust of what Paul wrote in 3:1-9. Note how the author brings this chapter to a conclusion.

> And this brings him finally to the great damage, the great harm, the overwhelming tragedy that comes if you let someone else define what you need to do in order to please God and be righteous in his eyes. (p. 82)

Going back to his criteria/standard by which the people should live "the better choices we will make and the better people we will become." Sadly, the author leaves the confusion, and his criteria/standard reflects exactly what he is urging them to avoid.

Another problem I had with the book was the overuse of illustrations. In some cases, illustrations seemed to take at least half of the sermon. I appreciate the need for and value of illustrations, but this seems a little over the top. For instance, in Chapter 8, "Working out the Working in," the first three pages are devoted to one illustration. In this case, I have to ask, does this help point to the main issue, or is it the main issue?

I wanted to like this book. I have spent considerable time over the past couple years studying Philippians. Yet this book is a disappointment. Overall, I don't think the book offers enough for me to recommend it, especially in light of the strong legalistic yet inconsistent approach to the Christian life. The confusion of Law and Gospel is evident throughout. In the process the author has subtly changed the focus of Paul's letter to the Philippians.

Sermon

By Rev. Phillip Hoffinga

Over the last couple of weeks the lectionary has been taking us on a cruise through a section of Romans in which Paul addresses the question, "What about the Jews?" The question arose because so many of the Jews rejected the Gospel even as so many Gentiles were embracing it. We cannot overlook the fact that, as a people and as a nation, collectively, the Jews had rejected Jesus to the point of delivering him up and having him crucified. As the Apostle John put it, "He came unto his own, but his own received him not." The question that had apparently arisen, then, was whether God had abandoned the Jews; whether he had rejected them and whether he had reneged on his promises to Israel.

And so Paul is addressing these questions and assuring his readers that God has not rejected Israel, but that God has in fact elected Israel, foreordained Israel's salvation, and He will be faithful to his promises to Israel. Nonetheless, because of Israel's transgressions, even as they are hardened in their disobedience, their sin has become an opportunity for the Gospel to be proclaimed and embraced among the Gentiles.

Now in chapter eleven, Paul concludes the case that he has been making over the last two chapters that God has not abandoned Israel. And at this point it may be helpful to point out the language that Paul uses for Israel. Sometimes he speaks of the Jews in very personal terms, calling them "my brethren, my kinsmen." Sometimes he speaks of them in ethnic terms, talking about the "Jew," or the "Jews." Sometimes he speaks of them in theological terms, as the "children of promise" or the "people of God"; while still other times he uses nationalistic terms, such as "Israel," or "Israelites."

However, the most important distinction for our text today is the distinction that is to be made between Israel as a nation, and individuals belong to it. It is important for us to recognize as we read this passage that the ancient mindset, especially the ancient Jewish mindset, thought of the collective first and the individual second. By and large, our thinking today is totally opposite. We think of the individual first, and the collective or community second, if we even think of ourselves as part of the collective at all.

The reason this is important for understanding today's text is that we need to understand that for Paul, the "remnant" is Israel, and Israel is the remnant. So long is there is a remnant, there is Israel. This is why God preserved the remnant in the Old Testament, even as much of Israel was destroyed or scattered because of its sin. "All Israel" then is not every individual who can lay claim to being a descendent of Abraham, but those who are faithful.

So the first thing that Paul does in our reading today is ask the rhetorical question, "has God rejected his people?" To which he answers, "No way!" Paul then proceeds to offer himself as proof that God has not abandoned Israel. There are, in fact, Jews that have not rejected Jesus, and Paul is one of them. I myself am an Israelite," he says, "a descendant of Abraham, a member of the tribe of Benjamin." And he compares this to God's promise to keep a remnant over against the prophet Elijah's complaint against Israel. "So too at the present time there is a remnant, chosen by grace," says Paul. But Paul wants his readers to understand that it is not because of any merit of his own, but purely by grace. Luther in commenting on this passage suggested that Paul uses himself as an example precisely to make this point – he himself, having been a Jew among Jews and a Pharisee among Pharisees had stooped to the lowest of lows in persecuting the Church. That Paul is among the current remnant cannot be understood as anything but grace.

Now Paul offers a second question: "So I ask, did they stumble in order that they might fall?" This is a very literal translation, and it's a bit confusing. I think the New International Version gets the sense of it correct when it translates it this way: "Did they stumble so as to fall beyond recovery?" Again, Paul answers the same way: "No way! By no means! Rather through their trespass salvation has come to the Gentiles, so as to make Israel jealous." God has a purpose for what appears to us to be a strange situation. The Jews, who ought by rights to have embraced Jesus, in fact are rejecting him in large numbers. The Gentiles, who have no right by birth to this Jewish Messiah, and who by rights ought to have no interest in him whatsoever, are embracing him and receiving the grace of eternal life through him in droves. That's the front-side of the matter. But Paul is saying that this is not just some strange coincidence, but that it is rather by God's design.

Remember that the Gentiles do not have the birthright. Neither do they have the Law. Nothing in them intrinsically suggests that they should come into the inheritance of the Kingdom of God, and yet they are being brought into the Kingdom through faith in Christ. This can only be grace. The Jews, on the other hand, think they can lay claim to the Kingdom of God by way of their own intrinsic merit. They, after all, have the birthright. They have the Law. Yet these things cannot save them from their own sins, from their own hardness of heart, especially from their own arrogance with regard to what they believe is rightfully theirs.

And so God has allowed their hardened hearts to reject the Messiah, the Christ, so that they too can eventually be saved by grace as they see the Gentiles receiving that salvation through grace. So Paul says in verse 30 and following: "For just as you were at one time disobedient to God but now have received mercy because of their disobedience, so they too have now been disobedient in order that by the mercy shown to you they also may now receive mercy. *For God has consigned all to disobedience, that he may have mercy on all.*" God has a purpose and a plan, and that purpose is to save all by his grace alone.

Now I want to pause for a moment and acknowledge that you may have wondered already more than once what this has to do with us. Perhaps you've noticed that there are no Synagogues in this small, dusty, western town. Some of you may have gone your whole lives without ever having known anyone who is Jewish. So you may be wondering how it could be relevant to your Christian walk. Paul answers this question in verses 17 through 25:

> [17]But if some of the branches were broken off, and you, although a wild olive shoot, were grafted in among the others and now share in the nourishing root of the olive tree, [18]do not be arrogant toward the branches. If you are, remember it is not you who support the root, but the root that supports you. [19]Then you will say, "Branches were broken off so that I might be grafted in." [20]That is true. They were broken off because of their unbelief, but you stand fast through faith. So do not become proud, but fear. [21]For if God did not spare the natural branches, neither will he spare you. [22]Note then the kindness and the severity of God: severity toward those who have fallen, but God's kindness to you, provided you continue in his kindness. Otherwise you too will be cut off. [23]And even they, if they do not continue in their unbelief, will be grafted in, for God has the power to graft them in again. [24]For if you were cut from what is by nature a wild olive tree, and grafted, contrary to nature, into a cultivated olive tree, how much more will these, the natural branches, be grafted back into their own olive tree.
>
> [25] Lest you be wise in your own sight, I want you to understand this mystery, brothers: a partial hardening has come upon Israel, until the fullness of the Gentiles has come in.

The theme of this passage, and quite possibly the whole reason why Paul has endeavored this extended argument in chapters nine through eleven, is contained in two phrases: "do not be arrogant," and "Lest you be wise in your own sight." You see, the danger in the question, "What about the Jews" was that the Gentile Christians might fall into the same trap that the Jews themselves had fallen into: namely, the danger of thinking that their calling was according to their own merit and becoming arrogant toward outsiders. And so Paul gives a warning in the form of a word picture. The image is that of an olive tree, which represents Israel. Paul's reasoning is twofold, but simple: if you, that is the Gentiles, being from a wild olive shoot, can be grafted in because some of the native branches were cut off because of the unbelief, how much more can you be cut off again because of the unbelief of pride. Beware! And at the same time, how much more will the natural branches be grafted back in if they believe!

Now I am convinced this warning is still relevant to us today, not because the question "What about the Jews" is on the front burners of our minds as it was for Paul's readers, but because we are subject to the same failing as his readers. How easy it is for us to look at people who live differently than we do, or who are lost, or who have fallen away from the faith, or who perhaps have never had faith; and how easy it is to begin to imagine that God has abandoned them because of their sins. And at the same time it is easy for us to begin to imagine that the reason we are saved has to do with our own merit. It is easy for us to imagine that God loves me, not because of the greatness of His love, but because, well, I'm not as bad as that guy over there.

When I was in college at Wheaton, we had a special speaker in chapel one day who gave his testimony. His name was Charlie Pratt, and he had been a hit-man for the mafia. He was arrested and convicted of murder and sentenced to life without parole. In prison, he had heard the Gospel for the first time through a prison ministry. He repented and was baptized. Though he expected to spend the rest of his life in prison, through a fluke in the system he found himself some years later out on parole. And so he went back into prisons as an evangelist to share the good news of Jesus with others like himself. What an incredible testimony! Later that day I had lunch with a young lady friend of mine, and I was still so amazed by the testimony I had heard in chapel that morning, it was all I could think to talk about. I asked my friend what she had thought about the chapel speaker. She was quiet for a moment, then she burst out, "That man should be in prison! He's a MURDERER!" She was outraged that this man should be allowed to come and speak to us.

Do we see others through the eyes of grace? When we look at our neighbor do we recognize him as someone for whom God has a plan of salvation? Or do we see someone according to the label of their sin:

that's a murderer, an adulterer, a homosexual, a junkie, a prostitute. It's far easier for us to pray, "Lord thank you that I'm not like that sinner," than it is for us to say, "there but for the grace of God go I."

But "God has consigned all to disobedience, that he may have mercy on all." This is the beauty of the Gospel. God is the great leveler, the great equalizer. Remember that God's covenant with Abraham was that through him and his descendants God would bless all the nations of the earth. So while Israel is the people of the promise, the effect of that promise extends to all peoples. God does not wish that any should perish, but that all should come to repentance, and all who come to repentance will come by grace alone – this is God's plan. And the gifts and the calling of God are irrevocable. For it is by *grace* you have been saved through faith – and that not of yourselves, it is the gift of God, not as a result of works, lest any man should boast. For it is by *grace* you have been saved through faith.

Printed in Great Britain
by Amazon

37276269R00045